The Austrian Subjectivist Theory of Interest
An Investigation into the History of Thought

Ingo Pellengahr

The Austrian Subjectivist Theory of Interest

An Investigation into the History of Thought

PETER LANG
Frankfurt am Main · Berlin · Bern · New York · Paris · Wien

Die Deutsche Bibliothek - CIP-Einheitsaufnahme

Pellengahr, Ingo:

The Austrian subjectivist theory of interest : an investigation into the history of thought / Ingo Pellengahr. - Frankfurt am Main ; Berlin ; Bern ; New York ; Paris ; Wien : Lang, 1996
Zugl.: Frankfurt (Main), Univ., Diss., 1993
ISBN 3-631-48607-3

D 30
ISBN 3-631-48607-3

Printed in Germany 1 2 3 4 6 7

Preface

The present book is the corrected version of a dissertation submitted to the Department of Economics of the Johann Wolfgang Goethe Universität in Frankfurt am Main in 1993. It is the result of many years of study and a debt is owed to teachers, collegues and friends too numerous to mention. I am particularly grateful to Professor Malte Faber of the Universität Heidelberg who initiated me to the theory of interest, roused my curiosity in Austrian subjectivist economics and acted as my dissertation advisor during the earlier stages of the project; to the Moorman Fund for financially enabling me to spend an invaluable year as an Austrian Fellow at New York University; to Professor Joachim Starbatty of the Universität Tübingen who repeatedly encouraged me to persevere during the many difficult phases of my work; and to Professor Bertram Schefold of the Universität Frankfurt am Main who generously acted as my dissertation advisor during the final stages of the project. My greatest thanks, however, go to Professor Israel M. Kirzner of New York University, whose unfailing patience and constant willingness to plough back to basics have to the present writer always seemed a model of scholarship which has been an inspiration throughout. All remaining errors in this book are of course fully my own.

Ingo Pellengahr, June 1995

Contents

Introduction

One element of modern Austrian subjectivist[1] economic theory that has proved to be particularly controversial even within Austrian circles (cf. e.g. WHITE 1984, YEAGER 1986) is the "purely subjective" pure time preference theory of interest. This theory is said to have been developed first by American economist Frank A. FETTER (1902, 1902a, 1904, 1904a, 1914; cf. ROTHBARD 1977a, 1987, 1987a, O'DRISCOLL 1979, KIRZNER 1980) on the foundation and in criticism of Eugen von BÖHM-BAWERK's famous *Capital and Interest* (1884-1889). It is said to have been taken up and developed further by Ludwig von MISES (1940, 1949; cf. KIRZNER 1976, ROTHBARD 1987, 1987b) and Murray N. ROTHBARD (1962; cf. GARRISON 1988).[2] The renaissance of Austrian economics in the last two decades has led to somewhat of a revival of the pure time preference theory. Exponents today include Gerald P. O'DRISCOLL (1979; cf. 1980), Roger W. GARRISON (1979, 1979a, 1985, 1988), and Israel M. KIRZNER (1976, 1983, 1993; cf. 1980, 1983a). Despite its controversiality, the pure time preference theory has recently found its way not only into at least one American mid-level microeconomics textbook (BAIRD 1982: 301-5) but also into the *New Palgrave* (EATWELL et al. eds. 1987), which, under the entry "Time Preference," reads:

> "Time preference is the insight that people prefer 'present goods' (goods available for use at present) to 'future goods' (present expectations of goods becoming available at some date in the future), and that the social rate of time preference, the result of the interactions of individual time preference schedules, will *determine and be equal to* the pure rate of interest in a society." (ROTHBARD 1987: 644, e.a.)[3]

In the present investigation we shall be concerned exclusively with the *positive* elements of the pure time preference theory. Our conclusions with respect to these will be largely *negative*: we shall argue in some detail that, whatever the merits of the general perspective on the phenomenon of interest suggested in their

---

1 On the appelation "modern Austrian subjectivist" for what is often simply designated as "Austrian" see Chapter 1 below.

2 Austrian pronouncements on the role of MISES and ROTHBARD in the development of the pure time preference theory are somewhat at variance with each other (cf. O'DRISCOLL 1979: 38-9; YEAGER 1979: 208; KIRZNER 1983: 13-4, 1983a: 221, 1993: 169, 171; ROTHBARD 1987: 645-6, 1987b: 480; GARRISON 1979a: 220, 1988: 3). As shall be implicitly argued in Chapters 5 and 6, if the theory is "attributed" at all to MISES along with FETTER, it should by the same token be also "attributed" to ROTHBARD. The arguments presented in the present investigation, however, suggest a radically different perspective on the history of thought. This perspective will be outlined in Chapter 8.

3 All emphases throughout this investigation are original, and all original emphases are retained, unless otherwise noted. In these cases, "e.a." will stand for "emphasis added," "e.o." for "emphasis omitted."

theory may be, pure time preference theorists have offered no satisfactory *explanation of the determination of the size of the rate of interest*; nor, indeed, have they advanced a satisfactory *explanation for the fact that the rate of interest is generally positive*. Much will be seen to depend on an apparent confusion in the very notion of time preference employed by pure time preference theorists - a confusion which may, ironically, be regarded as a result of "over-subjectivism." Yet, despite our negative conclusions, something of the theory will be seen to remain. This "something" may be called a "theory" or "explanation" of *the essence* of interest. We shall thus suggest a reformulation of the pure time preference theory - a reformulation which will not only be in marked conformity with the "methodological essentialism" Austrian subjectivists have traditionally espoused, but which will have immediate implications for a wider area of Austrian subjectivist economic theory, especially the subjectivist theory of price. If accepted, our conclusions will entail some reconstruction in the history of thought, Austrian as well as non-Austrian. Our investigation will also provide an example for the fact that paradigm changes in (social) science may not be sudden and revolutionary, but may instead be slow and go quite unnoticed by the scientists concerned.

To most, the negative part of our conclusions may not come as much of a surprise. Assertions to the effect that "interest is determined *solely* by time preference" (ROTHBARD 1987: 645, e.a.) and is thus a *purely* subjective phenomenon have invariably been met with raised eyebrows, if not downright incredulity, in the economic profession. The idea that the phenomenon of interest should have nothing whatsoever to do with "objective" productivity conditions is one that critics have found rather too obviously absurd.[4] Thus, even philo-Austrian Leland B. YEAGER simply

> "... cannot believe that the Austrians have a *pure* time-preference theory of interest (despite, for example, the praise that extreme subjectivists accord to Frank A. Fetter and Ludwig von Mises for supposedly having worked such a theory out).[5] ... (C)an anyone doubt that if the state of technology and other aspects of objective reality were much different from what they now are in fact, then the interest rate and the marginal rate of time-preference would also be different from what they now are?" (YEAGER 1979: 208; cf. 1987: 22)

So strong and pervasive has been this type of reaction that criticism of the pure time preference theory (where deemed worthwhile at all),[6] rather than taking the form of a critical examination of the reasoning offered in support of its *positive* propositions, has generally taken the form of a demonstration of the "indubitable"

---

4 For a characteristically apt and concise summary of this situation see KIRZNER (1993: 166-7).

5 Note that YEAGER makes no mention of ROTHBARD (cf. note above).

6 To the present writer's knowledge, ROTHBARD's exposition of the pure time preference theory (1962), for instance, has remained without response from the rest of the profession.

role of objective factors (such as technology) in the explanation of the rate of interest (cf. SEAGER 1912, BROWN 1913, KNIGHT 1941, MOSS 1978, YEAGER 1979). These assertions have typically involved the use of simplified examples, as epitomized in the FISHER-diagram, in which it is taken clearly to be objective productivity conditions that determine, or *co*determine, the rate of time preference and thus the rate of interest. Pure time preference theorists have as invariably answered such criticism by calling into question the logic (e.g. GARRISON 1979a: 144-7) or even the relevance (KIRZNER 1993: 173-9) of the examples proposed. In doing so, they have often echoed arguments against productivity theories forged by BÖHM-BAWERK in his *History and Critique of Interest Theories* (1884). These exchanges have not proven to be decisive. The present writer, who has made his own attempts to contribute to a solution of the issue (1984; cf. 1986, 1986a, KIRZNER 19893: 166n),[7] can himself testify to the considerable sense of frustration at the inconclusiveness of these debates.[8] It has been sensed to be a reflection of the "tantalizing conundrums" (KIRZNER 1983: 40-1) that have plagued the theory of interest over the centuries. Meanwhile, economists convinced of the fruitfulness of other aspects of Austrian subjectivist economics, and working on their development and diffusion, have continued to implore subjectivists to stop

> "... discrediting the sound core of their doctrine by contaminating it with bits of downright and readily exposable error" (YEAGER 1986: 29;[9] cf. 1979: 208).

The present investigation into the history of the pure time preference theory will suggest that these debates *may* have been somewhat misguided. It will suggest (i) that the pure time preference theory is not at all to be interpreted as a theory of interest rate *determination*; (ii) that pure time preference theorists have *misconceived* their own theory as a theory of interest rate *determination*; (iii) that pure time preference theorists are thus *themselves to blame* for this misguidance. In a recent "Attempt at Clarification," one pure time preference theorist has indeed - in response to discussion with the present writer (KIRZNER 19893: 166n) - admitted that the pure time preference theory has been misrepresented by its own exponents (KIRZNER 19893: 185). Our investigation will suggest an extension of KIRZNER's argument in at least three respects: (i) It will suggest that the pure time

---

7 An "n" following a page or chapter reference indicates that the reference is to a footnote. If the footnote is numbered, the number will be indicated after the "n."

8 KIRZNER has recently argued that the inconclusiveness stems in part from the fact that proponents and critics of the pure time preference theory have *implicitly* been employing different definitions of the phenomenon under scrutiny (1993: 176-7, and passim).

9 Note that this imploration can be found in YEAGER's programmatic opening article - entitled "Why Subjectivism?" (YEAGER 1986) - to the recently founded *Review of Austrian Economics* which serves as a research outlet to Austrian subjectivists.

preference theory has been *misconceived* rather than mis*represented*; (ii) It will show that this misconception goes much further than Professor KIRZNER has surmized; (iii) It will diagnose the source of the misconception in a confusion in the very concept of time preference employed.

Note that we shall *not* be concerned with a critical assessment of the "essentialist" aspects of the pure time preference theory themselves. To most economists imbued with a more positivist methodology the mere notion of a "theory" or "explanation" of the "essence" of interest may appear to be a contradiction in terms. It may thus be questioned whether such an essentialist endeavor should be considered part of positive economics at all. It is with the positive aspects of the pure time preference theory, however, that we said we would be primarily concerned. Moreover, the issues here raised would take us too deep into the questions of methodology and causality. They could be, and we believe should be, the object of a separate investigation. The present will be confined to showing that an explanation of the essence of interest was a distinct, although to some extent unidentified, part of early Austrian economic theory, and to suggest that it is perhaps in this tradition that the pure time preference theory should be understood.

In the following Chapter 1, we shall place the revival of the Austrian subjectivist theory of interest within the context of the recent renaissance of Austrian economics in general. This will give us occasion to make acquaintance with some interesting details concerning its wider context; we shall show in particular (i) that the pure time preference theory is by no means the only, nor indeed the best known, "modern" interest theory laying claim to the title "Austrian;" (2) that any *final* evaluation of the Austrian subjectivist theory of interest has to take place not only in the context of an evaluation of the Austrian subjective theory of value in general, but also in the context of the broader methodological tenets Austrian subjectivists have traditionally espoused. Chapter 1 will suggest, moreover, that it will prove instructive if we begin by retracing in as elementary a manner as possible the basic elements of BÖHM-BAWERK's *Capital and Interest* to a point where pure time preference theorists will be seen to deviate. This is done in Chapter 2. It is in BÖHM-BAWERK's theory that we shall identify a subtle distinction - one that went indeed unnoticed by BÖHM-BAWERK himself - which will form the basis for a later reformulation of the pure time preference theory. In Chapter 3 we shall discuss different conceptions of time preference considered relevant to this investigation. We shall then present and evaluate the positive elements of the pure time preference theories of FETTER (Chapter 4), MISES (Chapter 5), and ROTHBARD (Chapter 6). In Chapter 7 we shall add some remarks on more recent offerings of the theory (O'DRISCOLL, GARRISON, BAIRD, KIRZNER). With these, we shall have taken into consideration *all* contributions to the theory to date known to us.[10] In the concluding Chapter 8 we shall suggest a reinterpretation of the pure time preference theory, accompanied by a corresponding reconstruction in the history of thought. It is suggested that our reinterpretation may serve not only to unite subjectivists over the issue of the theory of interest, but also to render the theory more intelligible perhaps, if not more acceptable, to mainstream economists: Rather than contradictory, subjectivist and mainstream analyses of interest (and price) may, after all, be seen as fundamentally complementary.

It may be little known that Irving FISHER's "impatience theory of interest" (1907, 1911, 1912) was once widely regarded - by non-subjectivists (e.g. SEAGER 1912) and subjectivists (e.g. FETTER 1914) alike - as a subjectivist theory of interest. To the pure time preference theorists' disappointment, however, FISHER ended up sharply denouncing any such allegiance (1913; cf. 1930). On the reinterpretation of the time preference theory here suggested, FISHER's theory *does* fall within the subjectivist camp - in spite of the emphasis it quite clearly accords to productivity elements in the explanation of the determination of the size and of the positivity of the sign of the rate of interest. Since FISHER's impatience theory is not usually thus regarded, an evaluation of its relevant aspects is appended in Chapter 9. Our treatment of FISHER's theory will be submitted as indirect support of the central theses heretofore proposed.

---

10 We apologize for having to refer to some unpublished material, especially by O'DRISCOLL (1979) and KIRZNER (1983).

Chapter 1

The Renaissance of the Austrian School and the Revival of the Austrian Subjectivist Theory of Interest

What has been called *The Crisis in Economic Theory* (BELL and KRISTOL eds. 1981) has since the early seventies led to the birth of a number of new[11] and the *re*birth of a number of old and forgotten approaches to economic theory. Prominent among the latter has been a resurgence of Austrian economics (cf. HICKS 1973a, LACHMANN 1977a, KIRZNER 1981).[12] What had been known as a distinctive Austrian school of thought well into the thirties had fallen into virtual oblivion during the fourties, fifties, and sixties (cf. LACHMANN 1982; cf. KIRZNER 1987).[13]

But the Austrian economics that re-emerged in the early seventies was by no means monolythic. While all "Austrians" claim their intellectual roots, of course, in the older Austrian school of Carl MENGER (1871, 1883), Friedrich von WIESER (1884, 1889), and Eugen von BÖHM-BAWERK (1884-1889), two very distinct approaches laying claim to the title "Austrian" can be discerned. One approach is that of (modern, or neo-) Austrian capital (and interest) theory. It is severely attacked by what will here be called the Austrian subjectivist school, which claims to be the only truly "Austrian."[14]

Both approaches take charge with the inherently static (sometimes called *quasi*-, or *meta*-static; cf. GRAM and WALSH 1980: 121-41) nature of orthodox neoclassical economics (cf. HICKS 1979: 52, FABER 1986). Both, consequently,

---

11 Witness the appearance, for instance, of the rational expectations approach (cf. WILLES 1981).

12 In view of the characteristically anticlassical stance traditionally associated with Austrian economics, it should perhaps be noted that RICARDian (and thus classical) economics, too, had a renaissance during this period (cf. NELL 1981).

13 In his historical account of the fate of the Austrian school, LACHMANN speaks of the thirties as "a tragic decade for Austrians" (1982: 629) followed by "years in the wilderness" (1982: 630, 632).

14 Some Austrian capital (and interest) theorists (e.g. FABER 1986: 25n11) make a point of calling their theory "*modern* Austrian" (FABER 1979) thereby differentiating it from others for which the title "*neo*-Austrian" has been employed (HICKS 1970, 1973). The reader is cautioned that due to the claim mentioned in the text the Austrian subjectivist school often specifies its own (subjectivist) theory of capital (and interest) merely as "Austrian" (e.g. LACHMANN 1976). For reasons which will become apparent below, the Austrian subjectivist school has also been labeled "Austro-American" (e.g. in FABER 1986: 20, and passim). Sometimes, the appelatives "modern" or "neo-Austrian" have also been employed (KIRZNER 1987: 149).

seek an injection of time into economic theory. A seminal emphasis on the time aspect of economic behavior is located in the approach of the older Austrian school.

When (modern, or neo-) Austrian capital theorists think of their ancestry they think predominantly of BÖHM-BAWERK. The distinctive feature of their approach has been identified as the

> "... insistence on the nature of production as a process in time, with the temporal relations between inputs and outputs occupying a commanding position" (HICKS 1979: 51).

Surely BÖHM-BAWERK built his *Capital and Interest* (1884-1889) on MENGERian foundations. Thus it is for instance duly acknowledged (e.g. in FABER 1986: 13) that the distinction between higher and lower order goods goes back to MENGER's *Principles of Economics* (1871). But in general what needed to be revived of the Austrian approach after its near eclipse was BÖHM-BAWERKian capital (and interest) theory. Whatever else there once was of a distinctive Austrian approach was in this view substantially assimilated into the post first world war confluence of MARSHALLian and WALRASian traditions, the emerging neoclassical orthodoxy.[15]

Consequently, this kind of Austrianism focuses exclusively on capital (and interest) theory. While the importance of capital (and interest) theory for other areas of economics is emphasized (e.g. in FABER 1979: 3), it is not a change of paradigm that is proposed, but an extension of the neoclassical approach. The crisis of the latter is explained, at least in part, by its neglect of the time structure of production (FABER 1979: 5). And the neglect that descended upon Austrian economics in the thirties is explained by the difficulties that BÖHM-BAWERK's main tool of analysis of the time structure, the period of production, ran into during that period (FABER 1979: 29-33, OROSEL 1986: 23-25; for a survey of these difficulties by a participant in the capital controversies of the thirties see KALDOR 1937). The resurrection of Austrian economics, from this viewpoint, has to rely heavily on new formal-analytical tools.

Three (modern or neo-) Austrian approaches to capital (and interest) theory that emerged during the seventies have been distinguished (cf. FABER 1979: V, 1986: 21-5):

1. The approach of HICKS (1970, 1973, 1973a) has received most attention in the literature (cf. BURMEISTER 1974). HICKS is only in so far a neo-Austrian as he explicitly takes into account the time structure of production. He does

[15] While this may not be the professed view of neo-Austrian capital theorists, it appears to be a view implicit in the theoretical advances proposed by them. On the degree to which such assimilation has actually taken place, see KIRZNER (1987: 147-8).

not use BÖHM-BAWERK's concepts of the superiority of roundabout methods, of time preference, or of the period of production.

2. The latter concept has been revived by a second group to which TINTNER (1970, 1974), von WEIZSÄCKER (1971, 1971a, 1974), REETZ (1971, 1976, 1984), FEHL (1973, 1976), and OROSEL (1979) belong.
3. A third group, comprising BERNHOLZ (1971), FABER (1979), JAKSCH (1975, 1975a), and REISS (1979, 1981), reformulate the concepts of the superiority of roundabout methods and of time preference within a von NEUMANN-model and employ these to explain why the rate of interest is generally positive.

(Modern or neo-) Austrian approaches to capital (and interest) theory have been severely criticized from the perspective of the Austrian subjectivist school (LACHMANN 1973, GARRISON 1980, MOLDOVSKY 1982; cf. MOSS 1980, MOSS and VAUGHN 1982). This school, whose main exponents are KIRZNER, LACHMANN, and ROTHBARD, and whose intellectual center is New York University, also had a renaissance in the seventies (cf. DOLAN ed. 1976, SPADARO ed. 1977, RIZZO ed. 1979, O'DRISCOLL and RIZZO 1985; for monographs on modern Austrian subjectivism see SHAND 1984 and REEKIE 1984; see also LITTLECHILD ed. 1990).[16] The renaissance quickly attracted a sizeable following, mainly in the U.S., among which Gerald P. O'DRISCOLL, Mario J. RIZZO, Lawrence H. WHITE, Roger W. GARRISON, Leland B. YEAGER, Don LAVOIE, Jack HIGH, Karen I. VAUGHN, Hans-Herrmann HOPPE, Charles W. BAIRD, and many others. New centers with programs in Austrian economics have been set up at George Mason University (LAVOIE, VAUGHN, HIGH), Auburn University (GARRISON, YEAGER[17]), the University of Nevada (ROTHBARD, HOPPE), and California State University at Hayward (BAIRD).[18] In the wake of this revival, many of the original works of those associated with an Austrian subjectivist tradition have been republished in original or translated form, often by New York

---

[16] The renaissance was initiated by students of MISES' *Privatseminar* (mainly by KIRZNER and ROTHBARD) at New York University, after MISES' death in 1973. An *NYU Program in Austrian Economics* was set up in 1974. Ludwig M. LACHMANN of the University of the Witwatersrand (Johannesburg, South Africa) joined the faculty as a visiting professor at New York University in 1975 (and remained so until his death in 1989). The publication of a series of books related to Austrian economics (under the general title *Studies in Economic Theory*) was begun in the same year, and a regular *Austrian Economics Newsletter* was launched in 1977.

[17] YEAGER is "Ludwig von Mises Distinguished Professor" of Economics at Auburn University.

[18] A considerable number of colleges have also intitiated programs in Austrian economics.

University Press (see bibliography), and a regular scholarly journal, *The Review of Austrian Economics*, has been launched in 1987.[19]

Austrian subjectivists view BÖHM-BAWERK's capital theory with considerable reservations. Instead they look to MENGER (cf. HICKS and WEBER eds. 1973, ATLANTIC ECONOMIC JOURNAL ed. 1978), MISES (MOSS ed. 1976, KIRZNER ed. 1982) and HAYEK (O'DRISCOLL 1977) for inspiration. They fully agree with MENGER whom SCHUMPETER reports to have disqualified BÖHM-BAWERK's capital theory as "... one of the greatest errors ever committed" (SCHUMPETER 1954: 857n8).

Austrian subjectivism is not confined to capital theory. Indeed, the subjectivist criticism is leveled from what has been claimed to be "a paradigm truly distinct from that of the Keynesian-neoclassical orthodoxy" (DOLAN 1976a: 47; cf. GRINDER 1977). From this perspective, there is not much difference between neo-Austrian capital theory and neoclassical economics. Neither was BÖHM-BAWERK's *Capital and Interest* consistently "Austrian"; nor was the downturn of Austrian economics in the thirties due to the difficulties of BÖHM-BAWERK's capital theory. Indeed, "real" Austrianism was never *fully* assimilated into the neoclassical orthodoxy, but, according to Austrian subjectivists, lived on and continued to prove its uniqueness, particularly in the work of MISES and HAYEK. It was the dispersal and emigration of the leading Austrians in the wake of nascent fascism (MISES, for instance, went to Geneva and eventually to New York, while HAYEK had emigrated to London), the language barrier (it took almost eighty years for MENGER's *Grundsätze der Volkswirtschaftslehre* (1871) to be translated into English), and the sweeping victory of KEYNESianism over the MISES-HAYEK[20] business cycle theory (cf. HICKS 1967a, LACHMANN 1982),[21]

---

19 *The Review of Austrian Economics* is edited by Murray N. ROTHBARD, and is sponsored by *The Ludwig von MISES Institute* at Auburn University. The Institute now also publishes the *Austrian Economics Newsletter*, which was started by The Center for Libertarian Studies in 1977. George Mason University houses the *Center for the Study of Market Processes*, which is dedicated to the development of the aspect of Austrian economics indicated in its name, and the *Institute for Humane Studies*, which is also supportive of the Austrian approach. There is considerable cross fertilization with the *Center for the Study of Public Choice* of James M. BUCHANAN and Gordon TULLOCK, which is also at George Mason University.

20 Cf. MISES (1912), HAYEK (1931, 1933, 1939); MISES himself traced the roots of the theory to WICKSELL, and to earlier insights of the British currency school (MISES 1943).

21 LACHMANN reports that "(w)hen I arrived at the London School of Economics in the spring of 1933, all important economists there were Hayekians" whereas "at the end of the decade Hayek was a rather lonely figure" (1982: 630). In HICKS' words, the voices of the Austrians were "almost drowned in the fanfare of the Keynesian orchestra." (HICKS 1965: 185)

amongst other things, that triggered the neglect and near eclipse of the Austrian school in the fourties, fifties, and sixties. No doubt, *some* assimilation of Austrian ideas into the emerging Anglo-American orthodoxy had also taken place, particularly through Lionel ROBBINS' *Nature and Significance of Economic Science* (1932; cf. KIRZNER 1981: 114, 1987: 147); but this assimilation was never complete. Thus it was on the basis of characteristically Austrian insights into the nature of the market process that MISES and HAYEK were able to counter the LANGE-LERNER thesis, based on mainstream equilibrium arguments, that calculation of an efficient price system under socialism was possible (Lavoie 1985; cf. Kirzner 1987: 148). Some years earlier, Hans MAYER, successor to WIESER on the MENGER chair in Vienna, had already pinpointed an underlying difference between the Austrian and the mainstream understanding of the capitalist system by contrasting the *causal-geneticism* of Austrian price theory with the *functionalism* of the price theories of other schools (1932). It is the salvage of distinctly Austrian insights into the nature of prices and markets that modern Austrian subjectivists have put on the agenda.

In contrasting neo-Austrian doctrines, HICKS has identified Austrian subjectivism with its belief in

> "... the Supremacy of Demand, or, better perhaps, the Supremacy of Marginal Utility. This is not only opposed to the Classical ... determination of value by cost, but also to the Marshallian halfway house, in which both Utility and Cost play a role, like the blades of a pair of scissors, as Marshall said." (HICKS 1979: 51; cf. MARSHALL 1889: 569, 489)

This is, however, only one aspect of Austrian subjectivism. Indeed, the elaboration of MENGER's purely subjective theory of value was a guiding concern of the older Austrians, as was its defense against the MARSHALLian indictment that in overstressing utility the Austrians had erred at least as much as the Classics had erred in overstressing cost. MENGER had enunciated the doctrine and had, through his characterization of factors of production as "goods of higher order," laid the basis for its application to consumer and producer goods alike (1871): the value of producer goods is imputed from the value of the consumer goods attributed to their cooperation. WIESER developed the opportunity cost principle (1876: 380, 394) - the insight that cost incurred is nothing but a reflection of utility foregone by drawing the resources in question away from their most highly preferred alternative employment. With cost thus understood it was easy for WIESER (1891: 209) and BÖHM-BAWERK (1894: 361-2) to argue that MARSHALL's two blades were really both "of the same material" (SCHUMPETER 1954: 922; cf. passim) - subjective valuation.

What has come into sharper focus, however, in the context of the recent revival of Austrian economics is that Austrian subjectivists extend the purely subjective theory of value to the theory of interest. In this area, too, Austrian subjectivists oppose what they regard as the ruling co-determination parable, seen as shared by neoclassical economists and neo-Austrian capital theorists alike (cf. O'DRISCOLL 1979: 11), viz., the view that the rate of interest is to be explained by productivity *and* time preference conditions - a view paradigmatically exemplified in the FISHER-diagram (cf. e.g. SAMUELSON and NORDHAUS 1985: 665-7, FABER 1979). One problem is that this view, indeed, goes back to BÖHM-BAWERK - to whom FISHER dedicates his *Theory of Interest* (1930) - and that this is regarded by many as *the* enduring element of the Austrian contribution. It is in *contradistinction* to this view that Austrian subjectivists advance a *pure* time preference theory of interest (O'DRISCOLL 1979: 11).

The pure time preference theory is usually presented in historical garb (cf. e.g. O'DRISCOLL 1979). BÖHM-BAWERK is celebrated for his consistent application of the MENGERian subjective theory of value in his criticism of the productivity theories of interest, and for his "path-breaking" reformulation of the interest phenomenon as one of time preference. Yet he is chided just as much for his allegedly quite perplexing relapse into past mistakes by readmitting the productivity element into his theory, and by presenting what from this point of view is regarded as itself, after all, essentially a productivity explanation of interest. MENGER's dismissal of BÖHM-BAWERK's capital theory as "one of the greatest errors ever committed" is significantly invoked. The history of the pure time preference theory proper finally begins with FETTER, an early American economist, who criticised BÖHM-BAWERK on these grounds, and was the first to formulate the (then still "psychological") pure time preference theory, and to build a theory of distribution on it. FETTER's theory is judged to be "splendidly consistent" and to "fit illuminatingly into the broader framework of subjectivist economics" (Kirzner 1980: 8). MISES later depsychologized FETTER's theory, embedding it instead in a general "praxeological" framework of "human action." It is MISES' version of the theory that was taken up (and extended) by ROTHBARD, and by other economists identified today with the renaissance of Austrian subjectivist economics in the U.S..

The invocation, in this context, of MENGER's remark (as reported by SCHUMPETER) might be taken to suggest that MENGER's critical attitude towards BÖHM-BAWERK's *Positive Theory* was indeed provoked by the latter's alleged relapse into the mistakes of the older productivity theories - a straying from the path of a purely subjective theory of value (cf. e.g. MOSS 1980: 1098).[22] This view might be seen to be further supported by the fact that the time preference element in BÖHM-BAWERK's "agio theory" was already present in MENGER's *Principles* (1871: 153). However, so was the productivity element (1871: 152-3), as well as a description, although admittedly rudimentary, of the interaction of time preference and productivity conditions (1871: 153). And MENGER's own "use theory of interest," rather than being a purely subjectivist theory, was clearly a productivity theory,[23] and was severely (and rightly) criticized by BÖHM-BAWERK in his *History and Critique* (1884-1889, I: 170-7).[24] Moreover, it is out of critical reaction towards BÖHM-BAWERK's agio theory that MENGER later, in his notes for the second edition of his *Grundsätze* (1923), deleted any reference to time preference there had been in the first (cf. Karl MENGER 1923: XIV), and reinforced his own version of the productivity theory instead.[25] It has often been deplored (e.g. by WICKSELL 1924: 196) that MENGER failed to ever squarely address either BÖHM-BAWERK's criticism of his own use theory of interest, or BÖHM-BAWERK's agio theory itself. It should be clear, however, that MENGER's critical remark cannot easily be invoked as indirect support of whatever critical attitude subjectivists take towards the productivity element in BÖHM-BAWERK's *Positive Theory*.[26],[27]

In investigating the pure time preference theory of interest, we must be aware that it is part of the broader Austrian subjective theory of value.[28] But we must

22 Moss writes: "Certainly it was C. Menger's dissatisfaction with Böhm-Bawerk's 'third reason' that led him to describe the (Böhm-Bawerk's, I.P.) model as 'one of the greatest errors ever committed.'"

23 BÖHM-BAWERK calls the use theories "a branching off from" the productivity theories (1884-1889, I: 79; cf. 52)

24 Whenever a publication consists of more than one volume, the number of the volume referred to will be indicated by a Roman number following the year of publication.

25 MENGER had reinforced his position on interest as early as 1888 in an article "Zur Theorie des Kapitals" (1888), written in anticipation of the publication of BÖHM-BAWERK's *Positive Theory* which was to appear in 1889.

26 For a recent investigation into the grounds for MENGER's critical attitude, see ENDRES' "Origins of Böhm-Bawerk's Greatest Error: Theoretical Points of Separation from Menger" (1987). An evaluation from an Austrian subjectivist perspective, with particular attention to the theory of interest, is, to the present writer's knowledge, unfortunately still missing.

27 We note that MENGER did obviously not regard his productivity theory of interest as inconsistent with his purely subjective theory of value. This is no doubt due to the fact that he regarded his capital productivity as being "economic," rather than "technical" (cf. MENGER 1871: 130n, 1888: passim, 1923: 97ff; cf. 1923: 100n). Rather than being "objective", "economic" productivity is *value* productivity subjectively gauged by individual economic agents in the context of their forward-looking plans.

28 Strangely, the parallels between the two have, to the present writer's knowledge, never been investigated in any detail.

also be aware, that both are, in their turn, part of what we have seen has been claimed to be a (yet broader) "subjectivist paradigm." This subjectivist paradigm is usually contrasted with the "neoclassical paradigm" dominating economic science today (cf. Dolan 1976a). One of the outstanding characteristics of the subjectivist paradigm is what is often called its "methodological essentialism" (KIRZNER 1976a: 42) which is opposed to the "positivism" and "empiricism" neoclassicals at least officially (MCCLOSKEY 1983, 1985) claim to adhere to. This essentialism goes back to MENGER, who, in his correspondence with Léon WALRAS (JAFFE ed. 1965), criticized WALRAS' mathematical method as being unsuited to what he thought to be the main task of economic theory, which is to discern and analyze the (qualitative) essence ("das Wesen") of economic phenomena, and not their (quantitative) appearence ("die Erscheinungsformen"). In a letter of February 1884, MENGER wrote:

> "We investigate not only the magnitude, but also the *essence* of economic phenomena. Yet, how could we attain knowledge of the latter (e.g., of the essence of value, of land rent, of entrepreneurs' profits, of the division of labor, of bi-metallism, etc.) by the mathematical method? (JAFFÉ ed. 1965, II: 3, our translation)[29]

Closely connected is MENGER's distinction between "empirical" and "exact" laws (MENGER 1883). In contrast to the former, the latter are non-quantitative and not empirically falsifiable. In a previous letter of 1883, Menger had specified his own objective in a passage which can be found almost verbatim in the Introduction to his Grundsätze (1871: VII):

> "What I am concerned with in my investigations is the tracing back of the complex phenomena of the economy to their true causes ... and the investigation of the laws by which the latter, in their turn, bring about the complex phenomena of the economy." (JAFFE ed. 1965, I: 768, our translation)[30]

It is in this passage that Hans MAYER later identified the best description of the Austrian *causal-genetic* method, which he contrasts favorably with the *functional* method of mainstream eonomics - the latter being concerned not with the origin of economic phenomena, but with their quantitative relationship in equilibrium (MAYER 1932: 148). The Aristotelian origin of Austrian methodology, and the influence of Aristotelian philosophy on the founders of the Austrian school, has often been emphasized (e.g. by KRAUS 1905, KAUDER 1957, 1965, HUTCHISON 1973: 17-8).

---

29 "Wir untersuchen doch nicht nur die Größenverhältnisse, sondern auch das Wesen der volkswirtschaftlichen Erscheinungen. Wie vermöchten wir nun aber zu der Erkenntnis dieses letzteren (z.B. des Wesens des Wertes, der Grundrente, des Unternehmer-Gewinnes, der Arbeitsteilung, des Bimetallismus, u.s.f.) auf mathematischem Wege zu gelangen."

30 "Um was es sich mir bei meinen Forschungen handelt, ist die Zurückführung der complicirten Erscheinungen der Volkswirtschaft auf ihre wahren Ursachen . . und um die Erforschung der Gesetze, nach welchen aus diesen letztern sich die complicirten Erscheinungen der Volkswirtschaft wieder aufbauen."

This "essentialism" and "causal geneticism" of the methodology of the older Austrian school is reflected in the apriorist "praxeological" method embraced by almost all Austrian subjectivists today (cf. ROTHBARD 1976, KIRZNER 1976a).[31] Praxeology is said to "spin out *by verbal deduction* the logical implications of ... the primordial fact that human beings *act*, i.e., that individuals engage in *conscious* action towards *chosen* goals" (ROTHBARD 1976: 19, e.a.). Since the axiom of action itself is supposedly true apriori, the conclusions must also be true, unless there has been an error in the logical chain of deduction.[32] The theorems thus arrived at are non-quantitative, and cannot be tested by econometric means. Praxeology goes back to MISES, whose *Nationalökonomie, Theorie des Handelns und des Wirtschaftens* (1940) and *Human Action* (1949) consist in the application of this method to the explanation of all economic phenomena (cf. also ROTHBARD 1962). The praxeological method is geared not towards prediction and control, but towards an "understanding" of social phenomena in terms of their "essences" or "true causes:" social phenomena are thus understood if they are made "intelligible in terms of human action and the pursuit of plans" (LACHMANN 1973: 204; cf. KIRZNER 1976a: 41).[33] The science of economics traces economic phenomena as the "unintended consequences of such action" (ibid.; cf. HAYEK 1955: 39). We shall see this methodology at work below (especially in Chapters 5 and 6).

Before closing this chapter, we should perhaps finally take note of one further aspect of Austrian subjectivist economics today. This is its close association with libertarian ideology. So close indeed is this association that Austrian subjectivism is often simply identified with radical free-market economics (cf. MACHLUP 1982, SHAND 1984, KIRZNER 1987: 149). This is due no doubt to HAYEK's and particularly MISES' uncompromizing championship of the free market, and has been reinforced by ROTHBARD's prominent role in libertarian scholarship and advocacy. There are close links between Austrian subjectivist economics and various libertarian institutions in the U.S..[34] It may perhaps also be noted that the renaissance

---

31 As KIRZNER has noted, it is indeed in the area of methodology that "disagreement among Austrian economists may seem to be nonexistent" (1976a: 40).

32 "Praxeology" has also been designated as "extreme a-priorism" (ROTHBARD 1957), although this has been said to be a "misnomer" (Rothbard 1976: 25n15).

33 Pursuing a line of thought initiated by LACHMANN (1971), Austrian subjectivists have recently linked the methodology of understanding to GADAMER's (1965) hermeneutics (cf. LAVOIE 1986, SELGIN 1988). This linkage has been trenchantly criticized by ALBERT (1988).

34 Among these *The Center for Libertarian Studies*, *The Institute for Humane Studies* (which "serves a worldwide community of scholars who seek to expand the historical and theoretical knowledge, as well as the practical applications, of libertarian principles"), and *The Liberty Fund* ("established ... to encourage study of the idea of a society of free and

of Austrian subjectivist economics coincided not only with a crisis in economic theory, but also with a "new right" movement in social and political thought (BARRY 1983). Austrian subjectivists would be quick to point out, however, that whereas the older Austrian School by no means always favored an anti-interventionist stance,[35] MISES, HAYEK, and the younger Austrian subjectivists have consistently emphasized the "wertfrei" character of economic theory (e.g. KIRZNER 1976b, ROTHBARD 1976a). Their advocacy of free markets is emphatically regarded as a result, rather than as a presupposition, of their praxeological approach (cf. KIRZNER 1987: 149).

If the border between theory and ideology is nowhere as thin as it is in economic science, it is, within that science, nowhere as brittle as it is in the theory of interest. This is, as we shall shortly see, quite apparent in BÖHM-BAWERK's *Capital and Interest*. It is indeed against the background of the *Positive Theory of Interest* therein developed that BÖHM-BAWERK thought to have dealt a serious blow, on a scientific level, to Marxist ideology (1889: 341-6; cf. 1896). The Austrian subjectivist pure time preference theory is founded, to an extent yet to be properly determined, on BÖHM-BAWERK's "agio theory of interest." It is to an investigation of the relevant aspects of this theory that we now turn.

---

responsible individuals"). Some of the works of Austrian subjectivists have been published by *The Free Press* (Glencoe, Ill.), *The Libertarian Press* (South Holland, Ill.), or *Free Market Books* (Dobbs Ferry, N.Y.). Articles have appeared in *The Journal of Libertarian Studies*, which was launched in 1976.

35 WIESER, above all, came out strongly in favor of some of the interventionist policies of the German Historical School.

Chapter 2

Foundations of the Pure Time Preference Theory: Eugen von BÖHM-BAWERK's "Agio Theory of Interest"[36]

Little attention has been paid in the literature to BÖHM-BAWERK's *formulation* of the problem to be solved by the theory of interest.[37] Yet, this formulation is considered to be of some importance to the present investigation. On the very opening page of *Capital and Interest*, BÖHM-BAWERK introduces the phenomenon to be explained by the theory of interest as follows:

> "Whoever is the owner of a capital sum is ordinarily able to derive from it a permanent net income which goes under the scientific name of interest ... . It arises independently of any personal act of the capitalist. It accrues to him even though he has not moved a finger in creating it, and therefore seems in a peculiar sense to arise from capital or, to use a very old metaphor, to be begotten by it. ... *Whence and why does the capitalist receive this endless and effortless flow of wealth?* These words contain the problem of the theory of interest." (I: 1)

Böhm-Bawerk has thus limited his enqiry to the "theoretical problem of interest", i.e., the question of the "causes" (I: 2) or "nature and origin" (I: 4) of interest. He goes into some detail in distinguishing this from the "social problem of interest," i.e., the problem of the *justice* of such laborless income (I: 2), warning at length against the dangers inherent in an inadequate separation of the two problems.[38] Yet, he also significantly acknowledges both (i) the stimulus that the social problem traditionally provided for the investigation of the theoretical problem of interest (I: 3-4, cf. 39, 50-1), and (ii) "that there is no better way of coming to a correct decision on the question whether interest be a good thing, than by a correct understanding of the causes which have given rise to it" (I: 2). All the various "forms" (I: 5)[39] of interest, BÖHM-BAWERK proceeds, have their *origin* in the fact that the value of the product yielded by a process of production generally exceeds the combined value of the necessary factors of production; this "excess value" is thus called "*originary interest*" (I: 6). The phenomenon of "*contract* or *loan interest*," for instance, derived "if the owner (of capital, I.P.) foregoes earning the originary interest himself" (I: 6) by investing in a process of production, and instead loans out his capital, "is founded in all essential respects on originary inter-

36 References to the English translation of the forth edition of *Capital and Interest* will be by volume and page number only.

37 STIGLER, for instance, in his long essay on "Eugen von Böhm-Bawerk" (1941: 179-227) - the essay in question is the longest in his *Production and Distribution Theories* - does not even mention BÖHM-BAWERK's formulation of the problem of interest.

38 He illustrates these dangers with some instructive examples (I: 3).

39 The German is "Erscheinungsformen" (4th German edition, I: 6). Elsewhere, BÖHM-BAWERK speaks of "forms and varieties of interest" (I: 1; German: "Formen und Varietäten des Zinses," I: 2).

est, and can be easily dealt with in a secondary explanation, once originary interest has been satisfactorily explained. The explanation may therefore be limited to *originary interest*." (I: 76; cf. II: 299)[40] The existence of originary interest posed somewhat of a puzzle, however, in the context of the (then) newer (MENGERian) theory of value. BÖHM-BAWERK expresses this puzzle as follows:

> "If, as economists began to acknowledge, it is a sound principle that the value of the product is identical with the value of the means of production expended in making it, then ... (t)he one would perforce cling to the other with the fidelity of a shadow, and there would be no possibility of the sightest gap between them. - Nevertheless there is a gap. Why?" (I: 122)

BÖHM-BAWERK does not seem to be aware that *this* formulation of the basic problem differs from the above in that it involves the question *why there exists any value difference at all*, rather than *why the value difference is generally in favor of the product*. In another passage, both formulations appear together:

> "The theorist, then, who professes to explain interest must explain the emergence of surplus value. The problem, more exactly stated, can therefore be contained in the question, 'Why is the gross return to capital regularly of greater value than the portions of capital, which are consumed in acquiring that return?' Or the question can be worded, '*Why is there a constant difference in value between the capital expended and its return*' (cf. 1881: 107ff)." (I: 77)

The difference between these two questions will be seen to play some role in this and later parts of our investigation.

The undoubted *physical productivity* of factors of production, BÖHM-BAWERK responds to the productivity theories of interest so favored by "the majority of such writers as are not entirely opposed to interest" (I: 73), cannot explain the *value productivity* in question. For why should such physical productivity not be fully reflected in the prices of the factors themselves? ROSCHER (1854), for instance, posited the famous case of a community of fishermen in which one member, instead of continuing his daily routine of catching and consuming, say, three fish, reduces his daily consumption to two fish for one hundred days; he then uses the resultant stock of one hundred fish as means of subsistence for another fifty days in which he concentrates all his labor on manufacturing a boat and a net with the help of which his daily catch increases to, say, thirty fish. Interest, so ROSCHER, arises in this case because the owner of boat and net will be offered up to twenty-seven fish per day for renting out his capital; for, supposing that boat and net last for one hundred days, this is considerably more than the cost incurred in its production. BÖHM-BAWERK, however, retorts:

> "I grant without ado that capital actually possesses the physical productivity ascribed to it, that is to say, that more goods can actually be produced with its help than without. ... But there is not one single feature in the whole set of

---

40 Interest is offered on contract loans precisely *because* the existence of originary interest makes it possible to gainfully invest the principal.

> circumstances to indicate that this greater amount of goods must be worth more than the capital consumed in its production. And that is the feature of the phenomenon of excess value which has to be explained. ... Why should not capital goods that yield a great return be highly valued on that very account, and indeed so highly that their capital value would be equal to the abundance of goods that they yield? Why, for instance, should not a boat and net which, during the time that they last, help to procure an extra return of 2,700 fish be considered exactly equal in value to those 2,700 fish. But in that event, in spite of physical productivity, there would be no excess value." (I: 93-4)

Why, in other words, does competition by entrepreneurs (eager to obtain the profits from the purchase and judicious employment of boat and net) not bid up the *value* of boat and net until it fully reflects the *value* of the output attributed to its cooperation? It is this phenomenon of *surplus value*, however, that must be explained in the theory of interest.

BÖHM-BAWERK's own solution to the puzzle posed by the existence of originary interest pivots on the simple insight that the time dimension of goods matters as much for subjective valuation as do their physical and space dimensions. On this he enunciates:

> "*Present goods are as a general rule worth more than future goods of equal quality and quantity*. That sentence is the nub and kernel of the theory of interest which I have to present." (II: 259; cf. 265)

With the time dimension of goods thus put into perspective, the puzzle posed by the existence of originary interest (in the face of the newer theory of value) immediately dissolves. Means of production do indeed receive the full value of their product. Were they to be remunerated when that product is sold, they would also receive its full *nominal* value, and no interest would arise. Were they to receive that full nominal value, however, already at the time of their application, they would effectively receive *more* than the value of their product; for present goods are worth more than future goods of like kind and number. At the time of their application they thus receive the full nominal value of their product *discounted* by the "agio" (II: 268, 273) that present goods are subjectively accorded over future goods of equal quality and quantity (II: 300). Stated simply, this is BÖHM-BAWERK's "agio theory of interest" (I: 358).

Having enunciated the fundamental proposition of his agio theory, BÖHM-BAWERK immediately turns to presenting his famous three causes for this agio, and to setting forth the way in which these causes, via the agio for present goods they entail, work together in bringing about the various forms of the interest phenomenon previously distinguished. This is done in Chapter I (entitled "Present and Future in Economic Life") and Chapter II (entitled "The Origin of Interest") of his Book IV on "Interest," respectively.[41] The point we here wish to emphasize is that his conclusions as regards the nature of interest, the theory of distribution, and the social problem of interest, as well as his observations on "Interest under Socialism," drawn by BÖHM-BAWERK towards the end of these two long chapters, may be seen to be quite independent of any such laborious considerations. Interest is in BÖHM-BAWERK's conception a pure intertemporal exchange phenomenon. Since production, i.e., the transformation of inputs into outputs, takes time, it arises alongside the purchase, in exchange for present goods, of *any* factor for use in production. It thus differs fundamentally from the productivity returns (i.e., the rental prices) not only of labor and land, but also of intermediate (capital) goods (II: 299ff).[42] In fact, interest arises *whenever* present goods are exchanged for future goods, if there be no production whatsoever. Being merely the market expression of the fact "that present goods are for natural reasons a more valuable commodity than future goods," the phenomenon of interest is not itself reprehensible (II: 338). In fact, the exchange of, say, 100 present apples against 110 future apples is no more reprehensible than the exchange of 100 apples against 110 pears or, one might add, than the exchange of 100 apples in an urban location against 110 apples in a rural location (ibid.). The capitalist is simply the owner of present goods, who exchanges these for a *nominally larger* number of *less valuable* future goods (II: 337). From a subjectivist viewpoint no value surplus, no laborless income, is thereby coming into existence at all; for,

> "(b)uying a large number of less valuable future goods for a smaller number of more valuable present goods is no more a 'cheap' purchase than buying four $5 bills for two $10 bills." (II: 301; cf. 337)[43]

---

41 We note that whereas in his first introduction of the problem of interest BÖHM-BAWERK distinguishes two chief "forms" of interest, viz., "originary interest" ("ursprünglicher Zins") and "contract or loan interest" ("ausbedungener Kapitalzins oder Leihzins") (I: 6), he now distinguishes, without making reference to his previous discussion, not two but three "chief instances" ("Hauptfälle") of interest, viz., "loan interest" ("Darlehenszins"), "originary interest," and "interest on durable goods" ("Zins aus ausdauernden Gütern") (II: 290; cf. 290-337). In first introducing "loan or contract interest," however, BÖHM-BAWERK subdivides this category further into the case where the loan consists of durable goods, in which the remuneration is called "hire or rent," and the case where the loan consists of "perishable or fungible goods," typically money, in which the remuneration goes under the simple name of "interest" (I: 6).

42 Note that for SCHUMPETER this is indeed "perhaps the most important of all" aspects of BÖHM-BAWERK's agio theory, although BÖHM-BAWERK is said not to have brought this out as well as FISHER (SCHUMPETER 1954: 931-2). Cf. Chapters 8 and 9 below.

43 According to BÖHM-BAWERK, the misconception that interest is a *surplus* finds superficial support in the customary separation of the periodic payment of interest, calculated as a percentage of the principal, from the repayment of the principal (II: 297-8). While this has obvious advantages (in making loan transactions of different amounts and over different periods of time more easily comparable), it breeds the prejudice that the interest payment is a payment for the use of the principal, over and above its repayment.

Socialists intent on banning alledgedly "laborless" income extracted from the working class may succeed in banning certain more obvious forms of the taking of interest, such as contract or loan interest. Unless all forms of free intertemporal exchanges are banned - and this would imply the banning of practically all free exchange -, interest will accompany these exchanges in other less apparent forms, such as in the sale of any good of even the slightest durability for less than the full value of the services to be derived from it in the future (II: 342-3).

Of BÖHM-BAWERK's three *causes* for the preference for present goods, we briefly review his first two "psychological" causes. The first is that many people expect their wants to be relatively better provided for in the future (II: 265-6). BÖHM-BAWERK supports this by citing cases of temporary distress on the one hand and cases of an advancing career on the other (II: 266). He concedes immediately that there may be as many converse cases, submits, however, that in such cases present goods - and most certainly money - could simply be stored; in which instance, since present goods can fulfill present *or* future wants whereas future goods can fulfill future wants only, present goods would still be preferred to future goods (II: 266, 268n17). BÖHM-BAWERK's whole argument depends, of course, on the implicit assumption that storage is costless; once it is taken into consideration that even non-perishable goods, including money, cannot be stored except at a cost, there is no longer any reason why people who expect their future wants to be relatively poorly provided for should not be willing to exchange present goods against an equal or even lesser amount of future goods (STIGLER 1941: 213).[44]

BÖHM-BAWERK's second cause, the systematic and largely irrational underestimation of future wants (but not provisions!) (II: 268), is equally unconvincing. In addition to citing examples of human frailty (II: 268-9), BÖHM-BAWERK adduces three subsidiary causes: "(a) erroneous valuation by reason of fragmentary imagery of future wants, (b) lack of will-power, and (c) consideration of the uncertainty of life" (II: 271, cf. 269-70).[45] But again he concedes exceptions: his "fanatical devotees of foresight and providence" (II: 272) may serve as counterexamples to the first two subsidiary causes, and the admitted tendency to care for heirs (II: 271) casts doubt on the third. BÖHM-BAWERK's conclusion as to the re-

---

44 As STIGLER points out elsewhere, the *dis*agio of present goods cannot, however, exceed the cost of their storage (1966: 278).

45 This factor, so BÖHM-BAWERK, operates only for sufficiently remote future goods; but intertemporal arbitrage tends to make the discount on future goods continuous with time (II: 270-1).

sultant prevalence of a systematic underestimation of the future is merely asserted instead of being convincingly argued.

We may pass without further consideration BÖHM-BAWERK's third cause for the preference for present over future goods (II: 273-83), the "technological superiority" (II: 274) of present goods, and BÖHM-BAWERK's famous rule of the greater physical productivity of wisely chosen roundabout methods of production on which that technological superiority is based. Suffice it to note that it is in his third cause that BÖHM-BAWERK locates the kernel of truth of what, "esconced behind myriad errors, and going under the name of 'productivity of capital,' has customarily been dragged forth ... to explain and justify interest" (II: 273). Pure time preference theorists are unanimous, as we shall see, in their rejection of BÖHM-BAWERK's third cause (FETTER 1902, 1902a; MISES 1924/1959: 24, 339, 1940: 477, 1949: 485-6, 524-5; ROTHBARD 1962: 457n27) which is considered an unfortunate and surprising relapse into the mistakes of the older productivity theories.[46] Since we shall be concerned exclusively with the *positive* elements of the pure time preference theory, BÖHM-BAWERK's third cause need therefore not concern us any further.[47] This is true *a fortiori* of BÖHM-BAWERK's classically inspired, macroeconomic theory of the determination of the *size* of the rate of interest (II: 347-81) in which the technological element finally reigns supreme to an almost total neglect of his first two psychological causes. It is this part of his theory that leads BÖHM-BAWERK to the noteworthy conclusion that "the rate of interest depends on the productivity of the 'last particle of capital invested'" (II: 361),[48] or the marginal productivity of capital.[49],[50] As was immediately noted,

---

46 For criticism of the technical superiority of present over future goods, see also BORTKIEWICZ (1906), FISHER (1907: 53-74), and WICKSELL (1924). See also BÖHM-BAWERK's own defense of his third cause (III: Essay XII). ARVIDSSON (1953) also comes out in defense of the independence of the third cause; for a summary of the debate, see also CONARD (1959: Chapter 3).

47 See, however, Chapter 9 below in which we shall be concerned with FISHER's criticism of BÖHM-BAWERK's alleged technical rule of the greater productivity of more roundabout methods of production.

48 "Damit treffen wir fast bis auf das Wort genau mit dem berühmten Gesetze Thünens zusammen, welches die Höhe des Zinsfußes abhängen lässt von der Ergiebigkeit des 'zuletzt angelegten Kapitalteilchens'." (4th German edition, II: 457) HUNCKE's translation significantly omits the phrase "die Ergiebigkeit," and has here been altered to render original wording.

49 As WICKSELL (1893: 108-13) has pointed out, this statement is correct only in the equilibrium point; it is not true in the sense that additions to capital will secure a return determined in this way (cf. STIGLER 1941: 225).

50 The incomplete coordination of BÖHM-BAWERK's individualistic explanation of the positivity of the rate of interest in terms of his three reasons, and his explanation of the size of the rate of interest in terms of a macroeconomic model has often been emphasized (e.g. by WICKSELL 1928: 199, STIGLER 1941: 194-5, SCHUMPETER 1954: 927-8, LUTZ 1967: 10).

and as BÖHM-BAWERK to some extent admitted, this is clearly itself a (motivated) productivity explanation of interest (WICKSELL 1893: 86, PIERSON 1899: 217; cf. BÖHM-BAWERK I: 410, 410n112, 1911: 37n9, Schumpeter 1954: 931n19).

Reasons for this dichotomy have been identified in the divergent formative influence on BÖHM-BAWERK of the MENGERian approach on the one hand, and the approach of the German economists - BÖHM-BAWERK studied under KNIES in Heidelberg, and under the German economist SCHÄFFLE in Vienna - on the other. Theoretical economics in Germany - or what was left of it in a country so dominated by historicism - was still heavily under the influence of classical economics (HENNINGS 1972).

Chapter 3

Excursus: On the Definition of Time Preference

Whereas BÖHM-BAWERK provides no *formal* definition of the concept of an agio, or time preference, he clearly conceives of it, as we have seen, in terms of "goods of equal quality and quantity," implicitly including money as one of the goods to which the concept naturally applies. He is fairly consistent in his actual deployment of the concept: he applies it almost exclusively to goods, with only minor exceptions, such as an occasional application to present and future money,[51] or present and future utility.[52],[53] We have also seen (in the context of his first cause) that BÖHM-BAWERK regarded time preference as a *marginal* concept, i.e., the rate of time preference with respect to a particular good changes marginally with marginal changes in the relative provisioning with that good in the present and in the future.[54] This is important, of course, if levelling processes resulting from intertemporal exchange are to be considered (cf. II: 279-80, 287-8, 342). Last not least, we take significant note of the fact that BÖHM-BAWERK's concept of time preference is an *endogenous* concept, i.e., time preference with respect to a particular good is determined with respect to the consumption pattern chosen in the same manner in which, say, marginal utility of a good is determined with reference to the consumption pattern chosen.

Such an *endogenous* concept of time preference is often contrasted with what has been called the "modern," "neoclassical" version of the concept (cf. O'DRISCOLL 1979: 7-9, MOSS 1978: 160-2, GARRISON 1979: 142-3, 144), in which time preference is defined *with reference to a uniform pattern of con-*

---

51 "The discount to which our valuation subjects future goods is, as we know, by no means equally great for all future goods, but is graduated according to the temporal remoteness of its future utility. One thousand dollars that will be available as early as one year hence will be valued at about 950 present dollars; $1,000 not due for three years will have an estimated value of $850, and so on." (II: 302)

52 "Thus if someone, pursuant to his subjective circumstances, estimates a utility falling due next year at 10% below a present one of equal rank, then it will take a future utility of 110 to counterbalance a present utility of only 100." (II: 284-5) Cf. our comments below.

53 Note that, as his argument in the context of his first cause shows, BÖHM-BAWERK implicitly defines time preference with reference to *disposal* over goods, as opposed to the *use*, *services*, or *consumption* of these goods. This is irreconcilable, however, with an application of the concept to present and future utility. For the concept of disposal leaves it entirely open when the goods compared are going to be used. They might be put to such use that their respective utility would be derived at the same instant.

54 O'DRISCOLL's claim that BÖHM-BAWERK "adopted a non-marginal definition of time preference" (1979: 9) shall be considered in Chapter 7 below.

sumption over time.[55] Even if such an arbitrary benchmark is used, however, an individual cannot be unequivocally (i.e., regardless of the situation he happens to be in) characterized as exhibiting positive, negative, or neutral time preference. Firstly, even in a one-commodity world the rate of time preference might differ with different provisions with the commodity in question, i.e., in different realms of the indifference map (see e.g. FABER 1979: 77-8). Secondly, in a multi-commodity world the rate of time preference for any one commodity would moreover not be independent of the amount of other commodities available. Thus even a definition with respect to a uniform pattern of consumption falls well short of fully exogenizing the concept of time preference.[56]

A change in the definition of the concept of time preference is suggested by Irving FISHER. In *The Nature of Capital and Income* (1906), a book which FISHER says he had "primarily intended to serve as a foundation for *The Rate of Interest* which immediately followed it" (1930: 3n1), FISHER suggests that income should be regarded as ultimately psychic in character (1906: 165-79, 116-7; cf. 1912: 97-9; 1930: 3-5, 12).[57] Since such "subjective, or enjoyment, income" (1930: 3) "cannot be measured directly" (1930: 5), FISHER goes on to "approximate it indirectly ... by going one step back of it" (1930: 6) to what he calls "objective, or real, income." This consists of the objects - or, rather, the services of objects - "in the *outer* world which give us our *inner* enjoyments" (ibid.). Enjoyment income and real income "run closely parallel" in time (ibid.). Real income consisting of heterogeneous items, however, has itself "no common denominator" (ibid.). FISHER thus feels compelled to go back one further step to the "*cost* of living, the money measure of real income" (ibid.). FISHER considers the temporal parallelism between real income and cost of living to be still relatively close (1930: 7). Although cost of living is that homogeneous measure most closely corresponding to enjoyment income, it is not commonly regarded as income but rather as outgo (ibid.). What is commonly designated as income is "money income" which includes "all money received" (1930: 10). Money income, however, deviates from cost of living by the amount of saving or dissaving (1930: 11-12). FISHER summarizes:

> "To recapitulate, we have seen that the enjoyment income is a psychological matter, and hence cannot be measured directly. So we look to real income

55 Both O'DRISCOLL (1979: 9n6) and MOSS (1978: 161) have attributed such *exogenous* concept of time preference to FISHER (1930: 61-8). The relevant passages, however, contain no indication of such a concept. FISHER's concept, as will be presently seen, is as endogenous a concept as is BÖHM-BAWERK's.

56 On the definition of time preference, see also KOOPMANS (1960) and BURMEISTER (1980).

57 In the following, we shall refer to a concise summary of FISHER's elaboration of his income concept presented by himself in Chapter I of *The Theory of Interest* (1930).

instead; but even real income is a heterogeneous jumble. ... Here is where the cost of living comes in. As the cost of living is expressed in terms of dollars, it may, therefore, be taken as our best measure of income *in place of* enjoyment income, or real income. Between it and real income there are no important discrepancies as there are between money income and real income. Money income practically never conforms exactly to real income because either savings raise money income above real income, or deficits push money income below real income." (1930: 12)

In *The Rate of Interest* (1907) FISHER applies his income concept to the notion of time preference. Since goods are desired not for their own sake but for the sake of the satisfaction they confer, this notion, so FISHER, should be defined not with respect to objective "goods," but with respect to the subjective "satisfaction" derived from these goods, or, as FISHER calls it, generalized enjoyment income, as approximated by money:

"... (A)ll preference for present over future goods resolves itself, in the last analysis, into a preference for early enjoyable income over late enjoyable income. This simple proposition would have received attention before had there been at hand a clear-cut concept of income. ... Henceforth, instead of speaking vaguely and loosely of the preference for present over future 'goods,' we shall speak of the preference for *present enjoyable income* over *future enjoyable income*. ... (I)t is simpler to lump together these innumerable elements of income, expressed in terms of money." (1907: 90, 91, 94)

This definition also takes care of another problem FISHER has with BÖHM-BAWERK's concept of time preference, viz., that with that concept defined with respect to goods "*there are ... just as many rates of interest in goods as there are forms of goods diverging in value*" (1907: 84; cf. 77-84); this problem dissolves if time preference is defined exclusively in terms of *that* good which is chosen as monetary standard. FISHER's concept of time preference coincides directly with FISHER's definition of the rate of interest as "the excess above par which has to be paid for this year's money in terms of next year's money" (1911: 381; cf. 387, 1907: 3). Perhaps even more clearly than BÖHM-BAWERK, FISHER conceives of time preference as a marginal concept (cf. 1907: 92-3, 184). FISHER's concept of time preference also remains an endogenous concept, i.e., time preference is determined with reference to the income stream actually chosen (cf. e.g. 1907: 375, 1930: 303). FISHER emphasizes, however, that the rate of time preference between any two periods depends not only on the income of the two periods concerned, but that it "depends on the *entire* future income-stream" (1907: 92, e.a.). An explanation of the rate of interest in an economy, then, is co-extensive with an explanation of the intertemporal income-stream chosen by the individuals in that economy (1907: viii; see citation Chapter 9 below). We can thus readily understand how FISHER, on the basis of his redefinition of the concept of time preference, was led to reject BÖHM-BAWERK's distinction between the explanation of the positivity of the sign and the explanation of the size of the rate of interest:

> "It is therefore not necessary here to distinguish, as Böhm-Bawerk does, between the principles which lead to the *existence* of interest and those which regulate the *rate* of interest; for to determine the rate of interest will include the determination of whether the rate must necessarily always be greater than zero." (1907: 93; cf. 83-4, 1930: 13-4, 474)

FISHER's rejection of the distinction is implicitly emphasized in the very title of his *Rate of Interest* (1907). Indeed, on the basis of his redefinition of the concept of time preference in terms of money, the explanation of the positivity of the sign of the rate of interest poses no difficulty for FISHER whatsoever:

> "As a matter of fact, the rate may theoretically be negative, as in the case just mentioned of strawberries in strawberry season, or in the case cited by Böhm-Bawerk himself, of ice in winter. The reason such negative interest is not actually encountered in the market is that perishable articles such as ice and strawberries are never used as standards of value. We express our rates of interest in money, even if our contracts relate to strawberries or ice. But money possesses durability, and may be hoarded without loss. This explains why the rate of interest can never be negative" (1907: 93).

This argument is not convincing, however, as we have already seen in Chapter 2; even if durable, money is typically *not* costlessly storable. The rate of time preference in terms of money is thus not *necessarily* positive.

For someone less interested in measurability than FISHER, FISHER's attempt to redefine time preference with respect to subjective enjoyment income may suggest a more radical procedure. Time preference may be said to be positive if a present *satisfaction* is preferred to a future *satisfaction* which the evaluating agent happens to consider otherwise equivalent. Such a definition could be held to also dispose of the problem, encountered when the concept is defined in terms of goods of equal quality and quantity, who is to decide whether the goods, present and future, that happen to be up for consideration are indeed of the same quality. If one is reluctant to accept objective physical criteria as relevant for the determination of sameness in this context, one might feel *compelled* to resort to the subjective estimation of the agent who is to valuate the goods in question: goods are of the same quality if that agent considers them to confer the same satisfaction.[58] The redefinition of time preference in terms of equal satisfaction would retain the concept's marginal and endogenous character. But it would create another problem. This is that it is left entirely unclear how the evaluating agent is to separate his decision with respect to the equality of the satisfactions from his decision as to which satisfaction he prefers. The task is simply too difficult for anyone to perform: either two satisfactions, one present, one future, are considered equal or not. They cannot, qua satisfactions, be considered equal in one respect and unequal in another. A concept of time preference defined with

[58] In such scheme, however, the physical identity of the goods compared may be considered to be no longer of any import. The concept of time preference may even be applied if the goods under consideration are *not* of the same quality (and quantity).

respect to equal present and future satisfactions, however alluring it may seem to subjectivists at first glance because of its apparent subjectivism, is thus simply a contradiction in terms.

There may appear to be one possible escape from the contradiction encountered when the concept of time preference is defined in terms of equal satisfactions. Time preference may be defined not in terms of satisfactions considered of equal importance by the evaluating agent, it may be defined with respect to *one and the same satisfaction*. This would effectively re-reduce the valuation to be made to one: the question would now be no longer whether the agent does or does not prefer a present satisfaction to a future satisfaction considered subjectively equal; it would rather be whether he does or does not prefer to achieve one given satisfaction - say, quenching present thirst - in the nearer or in the remoter future. While this definition seems indeed to escape the contradiction encountered, it is no longer clear how it relates to the solution of the problem of interest as proposed by BÖHM-BAWERK and outlined in the preceding section. Moreover, such definition needlessly meddles into the question what use present and future means - say, present and future water - are mentally reserved for by the agent engaged in the intertemporal valuation of the good in question. We must take significant note of the fact, though, that the concept of time preference here considered is no longer a marginal or endogenous concept. The preference to achieve a given present end or goal (such as quenching present thirst) in the present rather than in the future is not touched at all by how far present thirst has already been quenched, and not at all by the extent to which future thirst is expected to be quenched.

If Austrian subjectivists have variously claimed that the pure time preference theory involves a *non-marginal* concept of time-preference (in contradistinction to the marginal concept employed in neoclassical economics), it may perhaps be the latter concept they have had in mind. We shall see that the latter two definitions of time preference are indeed *implied* in some of the pure time preference theories of interest to an evaluation of which we now turn.

Chapter 4

Frank A. FETTER's "Capitalization Theory of Interest"

An exception in this respect, we at once note, is FETTER's version of the pure time preference theory, called by him the "capitalization theory of interest" (1914: 230, 232, and passim). FETTER developed this theory most fully in his *Principles of Economics* (1904) and *Economic Principles* (1915) textbooks, in which they are presented as an integral part of a general subjective theory of value.[59] At least as important, however, are his many articles on this and closely related topics. The publication of a collection of these contributions entitled *Capital, Interest, and Rent. Essays in the Theory of Distribution by Frank A. Fetter*, edited with an "Introduction" by Murray N. ROTHBARD, was one of the early undertakings in the revival of Austrian subjectivist economics in the United States (FETTER 1977).[60] In the opening sentence of his "Introduction," ROTHBARD characterizes FETTER as "the leader in the United States of the early Austrian school of economics" (ROTHBARD 1977a: 1). This characterization is perhaps not uncontestable (cf. KIRZNER 1980: 8). Whereas DORFMAN (1949: III: 360-5) and MITCHELL (1967-9, II: 351-401) perceive FETTER as the leader of an American "Psychological School" - a description that has also often been used for the older Austrian school (cf. e.g. KRAUS 1905) -, SCHUMPETER evaluates FETTER as follows:

> "He was primarily, though not exclusively, a man of scientific progress and no friend to theoretical survivals. He has sometimes been classed as an 'Austrian,' but this is not quite correct. It is true that at that time all serious theoretical endeavors had to start from the bases laid by Jevons, Menger, and Walras and that non-mathematicians would prefer the Menger version to the other two. It is also true that he did not like Marshall - precisely because of the latter's attempts to preserve outmoded heirlooms - a feeling that was perhaps reciprocated. But all this does not suffice to make a man a *follower* of Menger. On that basis, Fetter erected a building that was his own ... . The vivifying influence upon the American profession's interest in theory of his critical exploits cannot be evaluated too highly." (1954: 874)

BELL also describes FETTER as coming

> "... near to being the founder of a 'school' which emphasized the subjective and psychological aspects of value theory along lines somewhat the same as those followed by the Austrian economists ... . Professor Fetter enjoyed great

---

59 For an early evaluation of "Fetter's Theory of Value" which emphasizes this aspect, see HOXIE (1905); for a Ph.D. dissertation on *The Contribution of Frank Albert Fetter (1863-1949) to the Development of Economic Theory*, see COUGHLAN (1965). For summary assessments of FETTER's views, see also DORFMAN (1949, III: 360-5, 385-6, V: 464-79) and MITCHELL (1967-1969, II: 251-301). COUGHLAN provides a complete bibliography of FETTER's writings (1965: 256-69), which is reprinted in an adapted form in FETTER (1977: 374-89).

60 It was the fifth publication in the *Studies in Economic Theory* series mentioned in Chapter 1n.

prestige as an original thinker and critic in the field of general economics." (1953: 644)

While FETTER himself described the Austrian economists as "hold(ing) the center of the stage" among the "utility value theorists" (1901: 75), he ended up being disappointed with their contribution (e.g. 1937: 159). His main points of contention lay surely in the field of the theory of capital and interest (ibid.). It is his own contributions in this area that put him within the first rank of Austrian subjectivist economics (ROTHBARD 1977a, O'DRISCOLL 1979, KIRZNER 1980).[61]

Like all pure time preference theorists, FETTER emphatically endorses (i) BÖHM-BAWERK's identification of the phenomenon to be explained by the theory of interest as that of the general persistence in competitive markets of a surplus of the value of an output over the combined value of the necessary factors of production, i.e., of originary interest (1902a: 186); (ii) his rejection of productivity theories of interest for being unable to bridge the gap between the undoubted existence of physical productivity on the one hand and the value productivity to be explained on the other (1902a: 186); and (iii) BÖHM-BAWERK's redescription of the interest phenomenon in terms of the value difference between present goods and future goods of equal quantity and quality (1902a: 172) - a phenomenon which FETTER originally designates as "time-value" (1904: 141, 145, and passim; 1914: 234, and passim)[62] or "time-discount" (1904: 131, 150, and passim).[63] Characteristic, as has already been noted in concluding Chapter 2, is also FETTER's poignant criticism of BÖHM-BAWERK's third technological cause (1902, 1902a) which he considers to represent a relapse into the mistakes of the older productivity theories of interest:

> "Critics of the Positive Theory have frequently declared in effect that while its author had ejected the productivity of capital from the front yard of his theory, he had opened to it the side door and had given it the freedom of the house. ... And yet this is out of harmony, first, with the author's own strong

---

61 It is perhaps noteworthy that FETTER - as was not uncommon among American economists at that time (cf. e.g. SEAGER 1893) - spent some of his academically formative years in German-speaking continental Europe. He must have been fluent in German, for he received his doctorate from the University of Halle in (1894). Later, he reviewed not only the original German editions of BÖHM-BAWERK's writings but also numerous other German language publications for the American scientific community (see the bibliographies in COUGHLAN 1965 and FETTER 1977). In later years, he must have kept close contact to the Austrian school, for together with Austrian economists Hans MAYER and Richard REISCH he edited a four volume compendium on *Die Wirtschaftstheorie der Gegenwart* (MAYER et al. eds. 1927-1932).

62 FETTER's use of the notion of time value is not always clear; at times he uses it to designate time preference as explanatory of originary interest (1904: 141, 145, and passim), at others he uses it to designate originary interest itself (1904: 151; 1914: 234; cf. 1914: 234n30).

63 In later publications, FETTER often also employs the notion of time preference (1915: 235, cf. 235-313).

> negative criticism of productivity theories as affording only incomplete answers to the interest problem and, secondly, with his formal statement of the theory of interest as due to the difference between the value of present and that of future goods." (1902: 89-90)

And again:

> "It has been a surprise to many students of Böhm-Bawerk to find that he has presented a theory, the most prominent feature of which is the technical productiveness of roundabout processes. His criticism of the productivity theories of interest has been of such a nature as to lead to the belief that he utterly rejected them. But evidently such is not the case. Critics have pretty generally agreed that the theory of the roundabout process is a productivity theory. ... (A)nd as such it is to be judged by the tests which he has set up, and rightly, in criticizing such an argument. ... Böhm-Bawerk has not bridged the gulf between the technical productivity and the surplus of value over the capital investment any better than those whom he has criticized." (1902a: 185-7)

While FETTER precedes FISHER in basing his theory on a concept of "psychic income" (1904: 39-45; cf. 1900: 53, 1915: 22-30),[64] this remains in his case without discernible consequence for the definition of time value.[65] FETTER follows BÖHM-BAWERK in defining time value basically in terms of goods (1904: 141), although his concept is initially broader than BÖHM-BAWERK's in that it encompasses intertemporal comparisons between goods of *different* quality (and quantity!) (1904: 141). This definition spells confusion, however, because it is no longer possible to isolate the temporal element in intertemporal valuation - a problem that is not greatly alleviated by the fact, immediately noted by FETTER, that in money-using economies goods of different quantity and quality at different times can be expressed in terms of a common denominator (1904: 141-2). Indeed, FETTER begins his labored discussion of time value in his earlier *Principles* textbook (1904: 98-169) by introducing money (1904: 98-107), preliminary consideration of which he says "is no longer possible to avoid" (FETTER 1904: 98). Unfortunately, his remarks on the relationship of money to the concept of time value are less than clear.[66] All this is again of little consequence, however, since

---

64 HOXIE considers the concept of psychic income "central and vital" (1905: 211) for FETTER's theoretical structure, providing no evidence for this view, however. Indeed, FETTER's view that psychic income is the ultimate object of economic activity leads him to regard all goods, including consumption goods, as means of production of such income (1900: 53-4; cf. passim). FETTER's precedence with regard to the notion of "psychic income" is acknowledged by FISHER (1906: 165n1; cf. 117). See also SCHUMPETER (1954: 874, 898n15).

65 It seems that one does not need a concept of psychic income to point out, as FETTER does, that intertemporal valuations are made with reference to expected marginal utilities: "What is really compared are various gratifications which may be produced by very different material things or services. In its last analysis comparison of values at different periods of time must be a comparison of psychic incomes, of two sums of gratifications." (FETTER 1904: 142; cf. 145)

66 Consider, e.g., the following statement: "The comparison of the value of a bushel of apples with that of a barrel of potatoes or a suit of clothes at the same moment appears sim-

his further discussion of time value here and elsewhere generally proceeds in terms of goods of equal quantity and quality (cf. 1904: 145).[67] In his later *Principles* textbook (1915), FETTER has eliminated all such complications from his discussion of time value (1915: 235-313): Time preference is here introduced as an evaluation of "present goods as compared with an equal amount of like future goods" (1915: 236), and money is only introduced at a later stage of the discussion of time value (1915: 262-72).

There are other indications that FETTER's views with regard to time value may have changed with time. Thus we take significant note of the fact that in 1905 HOXIE attributed to FETTER

> "... the assumption that it is a universal law of the human constitution that the postponement of gratifications decreases the estimate which is placed upon their extent. ... The discounting of future incomes, or gratifications, for time is a universal psychological phenomenon. To no man does the gratification of any want at a future time appear to be as important as its gratification immediately, provided, of course, that all other circumstances are identical. Different individuals discount the future at different rates, but all do discount future gratifications; and, therefore, all do attach a smaller present value to future incomes than to the same incomes in hand." (HOXIE 1905: 214, 221)

We note first of all that HOXIE is implicitly imputing to FETTER a concept of time value defined in terms of subjective satisfaction - or "gratification," as FETTER calls it - whether of the third or of the fourth kind distinguished in the previous section is impossible to tell. Considering FETTER's definition of time value just rendered, there seems to be no justification for such imputation. Nor does HOXIE provide any evidence for his general attribution to FETTER of the view that time value must always be in favor of the present; but while no direct evidence can be found in FETTER's earlier writings or in related literature, these contain no statements to the contrary, either. This has changed at least by 1914, when we find FETTER approvingly quoting FISHER's earlier dictum "that the preference for present over future goods of like kind and number is not, as some writers seem to assume, a necessary attribute of human nature, but that it depends always on the relative provisioning of the present and the future" (FISHER 1907: 184, cited in FETTER 1914: 237-8). Here it is also clear that he follows both BÖHM-BAWERK and FISHER in adopting a *marginal* concept of time preference; for he discusses the circumstances under which individual rates of time preference are brought

ple enough. When all are expressed in terms of money, the comparison of each with its value-equivalent at a later date becomes easy." (1904: 142) Neither it is clear why the intertemporal comparison becomes any easier if the two goods are expressed in terms of a common denominator; nor is it clear what the term "value-equivalent" in the second part of the statement quoted refers to.

67 In FETTER's causal-genetic analysis, the intertemporal exchange of goods is decidedly more fundamental than the intertemporal exchange of money (cf. 1904: 142).

into conformity with each other and with the market rate of interest through investment (or disinvestment) (1914: 238-9). FETTER explicitly objects against FISHER's later reversal in terminology from the notion of "time preference," as employed in *The Rate of Interest* (1907), to the notion of "impatience" (FISHER 1911: 387; cf. 1912: 371),[68] the reason for his objection being that he did precisely *not* concieve of time preference to be necessarily in favor of present goods:

> "Time-valuation or time-preference better expresses the complex of motives which at one time impel men to get goods earlier, and again leads them to postpone use by storing goods and by working for the future in many ways. A prevailing rate of interest is the resultant of all kinds and degrees of time-preference in a community, preference for goods in the future in some cases as well as preference for goods in the present, and it seems a great straining of words to attribute the resultant rate to impatience alone. Patience, self-denial, the quality expressed in the old term abstinence, have a no less important role in the explanation." (1914: 238)

FETTER's insistence that time preference may often be in favor of future goods is emphasized even more clearly in his later *Principles* textbook (1915), where he cautions that

> "(i)t should be carefully observed that time-preference is not always preference for present goods as compared with future goods. We sometimes, indeed very frequently, prefer to have things *in the future*." (1915: 237; cf. 236, 239n4)

FETTER explicitly mentions the ice-in-winter/ice-in-summer case as an example (1915: 237-8). He also notes that this is equally true of money, which "itself may be worth less now than later" (1915: 239n4).

FETTER significantly acknowledges that a *theory* of interest must thus explain *why* time value is generally in favor of present goods. The relevant passage, although long, is so revealing as a statement of FETTER' general position that it is worth being quoted in full:

> "Professor Eugen von Böhm-Bawerk's critique of the older interest theories marks a new era in economic thought. The highest point attained in his more positive discussion is his statement of the real nature of the interest problem, as that of the exchange of present goods against future goods. ... A statement of the nature of the problem and a solution of it are not the same. The English translater implies his belief that they are when he calls this statement 'the essence' of 'Böhm-Bawerk's theory of interest;' the author likewise appears to identify the two when, in his Positive Theory, he says: 'Present goods are, as a rule, worth more than future goods of like kind and number. ... This proposition is the kernel and center of the interest theory which I have to present.'[69] This, however, is but the fact which the interest theory is to explain logically.

[68] In direct contradiction to the statement just quoted, FISHER here asserts that impatience "is a fundamental attribute of human nature" (ibid.). We shall have occasion to scrutunize FISHER's reversal more closely in Chapter 9 below.

[69] FETTER is referring to the English translation of the first edition of BÖHM-BAWERK's *Kapital und Kapitalzins* (1884-1889) by William SMART. The first quote is from SMART's "Introduction," p. xix, the second is from p. 237 of SMART's translation, which differs slightly from HUNCKE's translation of the same passage, quoted in Chapter 2 above.

> The proposition is not open to question; it is a novel, but unquestionably better, way of stating the nature of the problem. Explanations may differ after the nature of the problem is well agreed upon. Böhm-Bawerk shows ... by devoting several hundred pages to setting forth his theory of interest, that he does not consider his work done when the proposition above quoted is stated. ... The conception of the interest problem as one aspect of exchange value must be considered merely as preliminary to the formulation of an interest theory, not as the theory itself." (1902a: 172-3)

In view of such pronouncement it is the more astounding that in all of FETTER's own writings there is hardly even an attempt at an explanation of a general preference for present goods (and thus of the positivity of the rate of interest). Surely, for all his criticism of BÖHM-BAWERK's theory of interest and especially of his third technological reason, FETTER nowhere takes issue with BÖHM-BAWERK's first two psychological reasons; FETTER counted himself (see e.g. 1914: 232 and passim) - and was counted by others (see above) - an adherent of a psychological school of economics; and elements of BÖHM-BAWERK's first two reasons do indeed turn up here and there in the context of FETTER's discussion of time value, especially in his earlier *Principles* textbook: here we find the cases of temporary distress (1904: 135-6) as much as those of a rising career (1904: 136), the fragmentary imagery of future wants as much as the lack of will-power (1904: 136, 144), and in his later textbook we also find the uncertainty of the length of life (1915: 241). But all this amounts to is only occasional *obiter dicta*, far below the standard set in BÖHM-BAWERK's already inconclusive analysis, and there is no *systematic* discussion of these issues in relation to time value at all. All this does thus not seem sufficient ground to attribute to FETTER an explanation of interest couched exclusively in terms of BÖHM-BAWERK's first two psychological reasons.[70] The nearest FETTER comes to an *attempt* at an explanation of the preference for present goods can be found in his later *Principles* textbook where he argues at one point that

> "... with all his foresight, and with all his appreciation of future needs, even the most provident of men is, like the animals, compelled to live very largely in the present. ... The needs of the present and the desires for present goods are, in much the larger number of cases, the more insistent. It is not rational (or even possible) to provide for the future until a certain minimum provision, at least, is made for the present. The typical or average preference of men is for present goods or uses. This does not mean that there is no desire for future goods, but simply that a larger quantity of future goods will exchange for a smaller quantity of present goods." (1915: 239)

And in an immediately following paragraph entitled "Biological basis for most choice of present use," FETTER proceeds to add that

> "(t)o take and enjoy things as soon as the desire arises and the means are present seems to be a fundamental trait of men. The impulse to seek immediate gratification is rooted deep in man's biological nature." (1915: 239-40)

[70] Even if it did, FETTER's theory would have to be judged unsatisfactory, as our assessment of BÖHM-BAWERK's first two reasons has shown.

FETTER's argument here seems not to be that time value is always *necessarily* in favor of present goods (cf. 1915: 239n4), but merely that man's constitution is such that *there is a tendency for the preference for present goods to prevail over the preference for future goods* - presumably in the sense that a positive rate of interest will emerge. As such it is as inconclusive as are his psychological *obiter dicta*. The prevalence of a preference for present goods is blandly asserted instead of being consistently argued. The fact that "the needs of the present are ... the more insistent" or that "a certain minimum provision, at least, is made for the present" does certainly not allow the conclusion that "the typical or average preference of men is for present goods or uses."

If there is hardly an attempt at an explanation of the general positivity of the *sign* of the rate of interest in FETTER's writings, there is even less of an explanation of the determination of its *size*. It should perhaps be noted, however, that, in response to criticism launched in his time against the time preference theory by the productivity theorists (SEAGER 1912, BROWN 1913), FETTER later acknowledges that a change in technological conditions *would* have "*some*" effect upon the rate of interest (1914: 247). But he does not let this detract from his pure time preference theory; for productivity, so FETTER, does not exert its effect on the rate of interest directly, but rather *indirectly*, through its effect on time preference:

> "... (T)he causal order is very different from that of the productivity theory. Technical productivity is one of the facts, physical, moral, intellectual, which go to make up the whole economic situation in which time preference is exercized." (1914: 247)

FETTER regards his belief in the causal priority of time preference as supported by the fact that, according to him, a rise in the physical productivity of all agents would not tend to raise (as asserted, for instance, by SEAGER 1912: 847),[71] but rather to lower the rate of interest:

> "That this, however, is not going over to the productivity theory of interest is shown by the fact that it points to an opposite conclusion as regards the resulting rate. The greater provision for present desires thus made possible leads us to expect a reduction of the preference for present goods and a lowering of their valuation in terms of future goods. This ... would be reflected in a lower rate of time-discount and a lower, not a higher, rate of interest, as the productivity theorist believes." (1914: 247)

As it stands, however, this argument is little convincing; for a general increase in physical productivity would surely increase not only the provision for present desires but also the provision for the future. But we have noted FETTER's own acknowledgement that it is on the *relative* provision for the present and the future that the rate of time preference depends. FETTER (1914: 247n59) does cite FISHER

---

[71] See also YEAGER (1979: 208), who has recently offered a similar proposition. Cf. Chapter 7 below.

(1913: 613-5) as supporting his conclusion; but FISHER's argument, also offered in response to SEAGER's criticism, differs from FETTER's; for among factors affecting individual rates of time preference, FISHER will be seen (in Chapter 9 below) to include not only the "distribution in time," but also the "size" of the income stream (1907: 94, and passim): the higher the general level of income the lower ceteris paribus the rate of impatience. It is on the basis of this proposition that FISHER argues that

> "... to double the productivity of capital will mean ultimately a much larger income to society than before, and this larger income tends to lower the rate of impatience ... (T)he rate of interest cannot be raised if the rates of impatience are not raised, and the rates of impatience cannot be raised if, as is assumed, the income stream is increased in size without being altered in other respects." (1913: 614-5)

This argument is, of course, considerably more convincing than FETTER's.

If judged by the standards FETTER set up himself in the passage above quoted, the conclusion must thus be that *FETTER provided hardly any positive theory of interest at all.* As far as such a positive theory is concerned, FETTER did not really progress beyond BÖHM-BAWERK's reformulation of the interest phenomenon in terms of the general preference for present rather than future goods of equal quantity and quality. Nor can it be said that FETTER's conclusions with regard to the theory of distribution (cf. e.g. 1902a: 187-8) point anywhere beyond BÖHM-BAWERK's.[72] On these grounds it seems that at least FETTER's *positive* contribution to the theory of interest has been not quite as unjustly neglected in the history of economic thought as Austrian subjectivists like to contend (cf. ROTHBARD 1977, 1977a: 1, 23, O'DRISCOLL 1979: 3-4).

Before closing this chapter, we note that although BÖHM-BAWERK took extensive issue with at least some aspects of FETTER' criticism of his own agio theory - he dedicated a whole appendix to a discussion of FETTER's (1902a) critical article on "The Roundabout Process in the Interest Theory" (III: 57-73) -, he never seriously addressed FETTER's capitalization theory itself. There is only the following footnote reference to it in his survey of "Recent Literature on Interest" (I: 355-432), in which he dissociates himself from FETTER's version of the agio theory:

> "Fetter himself espouses a variant (of the agio theory, I.P.) of his own, which he calls the 'capitalization theory.' This places him on the outermost wing of the purely 'psychological' interest theories - 'psychological' as opposed to 'technological.' He moves into a position far more extreme than the one I occupy, and even the one taken by Irving Fisher." (I: 359n14)

---

[72] There is, of course, FETTER's suggestion that the notion of rent be used to designate the rental price of any factor of production per unit time. This is largely a terminological matter, however, and does not really concern the positive theory of interest.

Chapter 5

Ludwig von MISES' "Pure Time Preference Theory of Interest"

Ludwig von MISES has been said to have been "the only major twentieth century theorist to adopt Fetter's pure time preference theory of interest" (O'DRISCOLL 1979: 38) - presumably not counting modern Austrian subjectivists (or not counting them among the major economists). As early as 1924, in the second German edition of his *Theory of Money and Credit*, we find a footnote in which MISES praises BÖHM-BAWERK for having been "the first to clear the way that leads to understanding of the problem (of interest, I.P.)" (cf. KIRZNER 1976). Yet, discontentment with BÖHM-BAWERK's solution to that problem is also expressed, together with the hope to publish, "in the not-too-distant future," his own self-contained study of the problem (1912: 339, cf. 24).[73] Unfortunately, such a self-contained study never appeared, so that we have to rely on his treatment of the subject in his larger *Nationalökonomie* (1940), and in his extensively revised English edition of that work entitled *Human Action* (1949; see also MISES 1940/1974). Fortunately, while these are directed towards an exposition of his own system of thought and contain relatively little debate with named authors (cf. Knight 1941), they do contain a full theory of interest. Indeed, his pure time preference theory is so central to his general edifice, and at the same time so characteristically MISESian, that KNIGHT, in reviewing *Nationalökonomie* in a full-length review article (ibid.), chose to concentrate exclusively on this particular aspect of MISES' theoretical edifice.[74]

Like FETTER before him, MISES clearly endorses (i) BÖHM-BAWERK's identification of the phenomenon to be explained by the theory of interest as that of originary interest (1949: 521-522 and passim); (ii) his rejection of productivity theories of interest (1949: 522, 524); and (iii) his redescription of the interest phenomenon in terms of "time preference" (1949: 521, 523). Like FETTER, MISES also laments what he considers BÖHM-BAWERK's own relapse into a productivity theory (1949: 524-5), although his strictures against BÖHM-BAWERK's third cause (cf. 1949: 485-6) differ somewhat from FETTER's. Indeed, there is no indication that MISES was at all familiar with FETTER's critical writings, his few references

[73] "Doch der Rahmen dieses Werkes erlaubt es nicht, meine eigenen Anschauungen über das Zinsproblem in ihm vorzutragen; dies muß einer, wie ich hoffe, in nicht allzuferner Zukunft erscheinenden besonderen Arbeit vorbehalten bleiben." (1912: 347n1, page reference to 2nd German edition)

[74] HAYEK (1945: 22) has been noted to have alluded to MISES as "the most thoroughgoing among the Austrians on these problems (of capital and interest, I.P.)" (KIRZNER 1976: 51).

to FETTER (1940: 260, 443, 1949: 262, 271, 486, 631) being either to his two *Principles* textbooks or to his later contributions to the *Encyclopedia of the Social Sciences* on the subjects of "Capital" (1930-1935) and "Rent" (1930-1935a). MISES goes beyond FETTER's criticism of BÖHM-BAWERK's *Positive Theory* in that his criticism encompasses, as we shall see, a rejection also of BÖHM-BAWERK's first two psychological reasons. Yet, in spite of his apparent familiarity with FETTER's theory of interest and the scope of his criticism of BÖHM-BAWERK's *Positive Theory*, in his "Observations on the Evolution of the Time-Preference Theory" MISES mentions BÖHM-BAWERK rather than FETTER as founder of the time preference theory of interest:

> "Economics owes the time-preference theory to William Stanley Jevons and its elaboration, most of all, to Eugen von Böhm-Bawerk. ... It was on the foundation laid by him that later economists - foremost among them Knut Wicksell, Frank Albert Fetter, and Irving Fisher - were successful in perfecting the time-preference theory." (1949: 485-6; cf. 479)[75],[76]

In spite of the importance MISES attaches to time and time preference in his own theoretical structure (cf. 1949: chs. XVIII-XIX), it is not at all easy to find out what he means by "time preference." Thus, no formal definition of the concept is provided (1949: 480ff). MISES often expresses time preference vaguely in terms of a comparison of present (or earlier) and future (or later) *satisfaction* (1949: 480, 481, 483, 484, 487, 490, 523, 526, 529); but nowhere does he explicitly specify conditions concerning the satisfactions compared. There are also passages in which MISES expresses time preference in terms of present and future *goods* (1949: 481, 486, 521, 522, 523, 524, 528, 529, 530), and others again in which he refers to a comparison of present and future consumption (1949: 483, 487), uses (1949: 486), or services (1949: 480) - as opposed to disposal - of goods; but then he says that it is only "customary to express the essence of the time preference theory" in "this mode of expression" (1949: 486), and again there is no explicit specification of the conditions attached to the goods thus compared.[77] The ambiguity between a definition of time preference in terms of

75 Unfortunately, MISES fails to specify in what this "perfecting" consisted.

76 Since in all of the Austrian subjectivist literature concerned this is the only mentioning of JEVONS and WICKSELL in the context of the pure time preference theory of interest, their contributions have not been included in the present investigation. The mention of WICKSELL may perhaps appear particularly astounding, since WICKSELL, as well as KNIGHT, emphasized almost exclusively the productivity factor in the explanation of interest (cf. HAYEK 1945: 22). As will be seen in Chapter 9, FISHER also emphasized the productivity element. If by "perfecting the time-preference theory" MISES meant "freeing it from the productivity elements readmitted so freely by BÖHM-BAWERK," neither WICKSELL nor FISHER should properly be mentioned. An interpretation of MISES' inclusion of WICKSELL and FISHER will be suggested in Chapter 9 below.

77 For instance, their being "of equal quantity and quality."

subjective satisfaction and a definition in terms of objective goods is contained also in a passage that perhaps comes closest to constituting a *definition* of the concept. MISES here writes:

> "Satisfaction of a want in the nearer future is, other things being equal, preferred to that in the farther distant future. Present goods are more valuable than future goods." (1949: 480-1)

Finally, there are also passages in which time preference is expressed in terms of money (1949: 483, 528, 529); but once again the preference for present over future money seems to be rather a manifestation of some deeper meaning attached to the concept. In order to find out more about that deeper meaning, we turn to an evaluation of MISES' peculiar answer to the question why time preference is generally in favor of present rather than future goods or satisfations.

Before doing so it will prove convenient, however, if we retrace briefly MISES' criticism of BÖHM-BAWERK's first two psychological causes.[78] This criticism is contained in MISES' *Nationalökonomie* (1940: 439-43), but is only briefly summarized in MISES' *Human Action* (1949: 485), with a footnote (1949: 485n5) referring the reader to the earlier German text. A translation of the relevant passage (MISES 1940/1974) has appeared, however, in GREAVES (1974: 150-157). Offering extensive counterexamples to each of BÖHM-BAWERK's first two reasons and taking significant note of the fact that BÖHM-BAWERK had himself admitted such counterexamples (cf. Chapter 2 above), MISES here argues that

> "Böhm-Bawerk's error consisted primarily in the fact that he sought to base the theory of the higher valuation of present goods on psychological grounds. However, a universally true theory may never be attained via psychological paths. Psychology can show us that some persons, or even many persons, are guided by certain influences. But psychology can never demonstrate that a definite conduct is necessarily always and in the same way common to all men. As a matter of fact, what Böhm-Bawerk actually succeeds in demonstrating is only that it appears plausible for men to place higher values on present goods than future goods under some circumstances, while under other circumstances it appears no less plausible for the opposite to be true, i.e., for future goods to be more highly valued than present goods." (MISES 1940/1974: 156; cf. 1940: 443, 1949: 485)

We are not here concerned with an evaluation of this reasoning in and of itself; such an evaluation depends in part on MISES' success in demonstrating that "a universally true theory" of "the higher valuation of present goods" really exists. We merely want to argue that insofar as FETTER may be said to have offered an explanation of the positivity of the rate of interest based on psychological consid-

[78] Since this criticism must be considered an indirect criticism of FETTER's capitalization theory, it must also be considered of relevance to the positive elements of the pure time preference theory.

erations (cf. Chapter 4), MISES would hardly have been prepared to accepted it.[79] We also note that in all of his elaborate and detailed criticism of BÖHM-BAWERK's first two reasons, MISES ignores its possibly most nearly convincing (and least "psychological") element, viz., BÖHM-BAWERK's argument, offered in the context of his first reason, that in money economies present goods are always preferred because their money equivalent can be costlessly stored (cf. Chapter 2 above).[80]

Unlike FETTER, MISES follows BÖHM-BAWERK in squarely addressing the question why time preference is generally in favor of present (or earlier) rather than future (or later) "goods" or "satisfactions" and thus why the rate of interest is generally positive. In a section entitled "Time Preference as an Essential Requisite of Action" (1949: 480-5), MISES argues that since human action is always directed at the satisfaction of some desire, the very fact that agents do act (presumably as opposed to deferring action) implies that earlier satisfaction is preferred to later satisfaction. Time preference, for MISES, is thus neither the result of human psychology (1949: 483) nor physiology (1949: 483-4); instead,

> "(t)ime preference is a categorial requisite of human action. No mode of action can be thought of in which satisfaction within a nearer period of the future is not - other things being equal - preferred to that in a later period. The

79 MISES did not comment upon the psychological elements in FETTER's capitalization theory, in spite of his apparent familiarity with FETTER's *Principles* textbooks, in which, as we have argued, these psychological elements can be discerned.

80 The reader must not be confused by KNIGHT's misleading characterization of MISES' position on interest, which is contained in the following passage: "In saying that Professor Mises is a defender of Böhm-Bawerk's theory of capital, it is necessary to introduce at once an important qualification. He is a defender of the general theory or principle which Böhm-Bawerk announces as ... the basis of interest, namely that men place a higher value on present than on future goods or satisfactions. Böhm-Bawerk himself, as readers will recall, gave three grounds for this preference. The first ground, the relation between want and provision for want in present versus future, is here definitely repudiated - quite rightly as I believe. ... More important is the fact that Mises definitely rejects the third ground, the famous superior productivity of technical roundabout methods of production (*Mehrergiebigkeit der Umwege*) which Böhm-Bawerk finally made the basis of his own theory of capital and interest, in all the latter part of his work. He (Mises) will have nothing to do with the 'productivity' theory of capital in any form, including explicitly that of Böhm-Bawerk, as the basis for interest. Thus the position which he actually defends is that of Böhm-Bawerk's second (the original mistakenly reads "first," I.P.) ground ... which makes the preference in question an ultimate fact of preference (a *Wertung*, in Mises' terminology). This is the theory associated with the name of Professor Fetter (though Mises has no inclination to call it by Fetter's designation, a 'psychological' theory) and which Professor Fetter, and critics in general (and I believe rightly), contrast with 'the' position of Böhm-Bawerk." (1941: 411-2) MISES clearly rejects BÖHM-BAWERK's second ground as definitely as his first, and insofar as FETTER's position must be interpreted as incorporating BÖHM-BAWERK's psychological grounds, it must clearly be interpreted as incorporating *both*.

very act of gratifying a desire implies that gratification at the present instant is preferred to that at a later instant." (1949: 481)[81]

MISES immediately goes on to apply this argument to goods, consumption (or use) of which (presumably as opposed to storage) he regards as proof of the fact that present goods (or services) are preferred over the same quantity of future goods (or services):

> "He who consumes a nonperishable good instead of postponing consumption to an indefinite later moment thereby reveals a higher valuation of present satisfaction as compared with later satisfaction. If he were not to prefer satisfaction in a nearer period of the future to that in a remoter period, he would never consume and so satisfy wants. He would always accumulate, he would never consume and enjoy. He would not consume today, but he would not consume tomorrow either, as the morrow would confront him with the same alternative." (1949: 481; cf. 483, 487)

The case here considered is what MISES calls "the case of plain saving in which people must choose between the immediate consumption of a quantity of goods and the later consumption of the same quantity" (1949: 483). He goes on to consider "the case of capitalist saving in which the choice is to be made between the immediate consumption of a quantity of goods and the later consumption ... of a *greater* quantity" (ibid., e.a.). In this context of a "capitalist economy," MISES inadvertantly switches to arguing in terms of money:

> "Those contesting the universal validity of time preference fail to explain why a man does not always invest a sum of 100 dollars available today, although these 100 dollars would increase to 104 dollars in a year's time. It is obvious that this man in consuming this sum today is determined by a judgement of value which values 100 present dollars higher than 104 dollars available a year later. But even in case he chooses to invest these 100 dollars, the meaning is not that he prefers satisfaction in a later period to that of today. It means that he values 100 dollars today less than 104 dollars a year later. Every penny spent today is, precisely under the condition of a capitalist economy in which institutions make it possible to invest even the smallest sums, a proof of the higher valuation of present satisfaction as compared with later satisfaction." (1949: 483)

The proof having been provided for both the case of plain and the case of capitalist saving, MISES takes his proposition as conclusively established: "No other case is thinkable." (1949: 483)

There are substantial problems, however, with each part of this reasoning. MISES' basic argument, designed to show that earlier satisfaction is always preferred over later satisfaction, suffers from the fact that in some cases, action is in fact deferred - indeed, actions that we observe may have been deferred earlier - only that deferment of an action is not observable in the same way in which non-

---

[81] In the corresponding passage of MISES' *Nationalökonomie* (1940: 443) a footnote reference to FETTER's *Principles of Economics* (1904: 443ff) can be found, obviously attributing a similar argument to FETTER. Yet, perusal of the relevant passages reveals no justification whatsoever for such attribution. We recall, however, that HOXIE (1905: 214, 221) already attributed such argument to FETTER (see Chapter 4 above).

deferment is observable. In cases of deferment, however, later satisfaction would have to be considered preferred over earlier by the same token by which in the case of non-deferment earlier satisfaction is considered preferred over later. No obvious inference can thus be drawn from human action for the relative valuation of present and future satisfaction. Moreover, it is not clear what meaning we are to attach to the proposition that earlier satisfaction is preferred over later satisfaction. Non-deferment of action obviously implies that the satisfaction derived from action is considered greater than the satisfaction derived from deferment of action. But then the two satisfactions are plainly not equivalent. Are they to be considered equivalent in all but their time-dimension? Then how is equivalence in all but time-dimension determined? Or are they perhaps to be considered to be actually one and the same satisfaction, such as quenching present thirst now or later. Then how are we to interpret situations in which choice between deferment and non-deferment is made in quite another context? And even if these questions could be satisfactorily answered, there remains the further question as to the relation between time preference thus defined and the phenomenon of originary interest.

MISES' application of his general argument to the category of goods fares no better. His reasoning applies only to goods that are both nonperishable and costlessly storable. Indeed, MISES mentions nonperishability once as an assumption (in the passage above cited); but in dealing with the notorious ice-in-winter/ice-in-summer counterexample he adopts the following somewhat different strategy:

> "(A) seeming exception is presented by the case of perishable goods. They may be available in abundance in one season of the year and may be scarce in other seasons. However, the difference between ice in winter and ice in summer is not that between a present good and a future good. It is the difference between a good that looses its specific usefulness even if not consumed and another good which requires a different process of production. Ice available in winter can only be used in summer when subjected to a special process of conservation. It is, in respect to ice utilizable in summer, at best one of the complementary factors required for production. It is impossible to increase the quantity of ice available in summer simply by restricting the consumption of ice in winter. The two things are for all practical purposes different commodities." (1949: 486-7)[82]

Physically (and spatially) identical goods available at different points of time thus counting as commodities of the same quality only if they are also nonperishable, nonperishability would have to enter no longer as an additional assumption into the comparison of present and future goods of equal quantity and quality. Introduction of the assumption of costless storability, necessary but neglected by

[82] Note that MISES here introduces a characteristically objectivist, backward-looking, production-oriented criterion for determining whether goods are to be considered of the same quality. In contrast to MISES, ROTHBARD will be seen to introduce a forward-looking subjectivist criterion in dealing with the same problem (cf. Chapter 6).

MISES, limits the scope of MISES' proposition still further. Needless to say, a concept of time preference thus restricted is of dubious value for an explanation of the phenomenon of interest.[83] But this is not the only problem with MISES' proposition, nor is it the most serious. MISES' argument may be simply reversed, to prove the opposite conclusion: one only needs to consider the case where a (nonperishable, costlessly storable) good *is* indeed stored! The problem with MISES' "case of plain saving" is that under MISES' assumptions the goods available will be so allocated to present and future consumption that with respect to the last unit consumed it is true that the present is preferred over the future good, whereas with respect to the first unit stored it is true that the future good is preferred over the present good. All that MISES' case of plain saving can thus prove is that, at the margin, a present unit of the good in question is considered roughly equal in value to a future unit of the same good. This is paradoxically rather a result of the *objective* conditions assumed by MISES, i.e., of the fact that the only possibility of transforming present into future goods is storage (or, in terms of a single-commodity FISHER-diagram, that the absolute value of the slope of the opportunity curve is assumed everywhere equal to unity).

The same stricture applies in MISES' "case of capitalist saving," which is couched in terms of the preference for present over future *money*. In assuming the existence of the possibility of transforming 100 units of present money into 104 units of future money (or vice versa) at will, MISES assumes objective conditions (i.e., an absolute value of the slope of the opportunity curve in the FISHER-diagram of 1.04) that are such that the rate of time preference in terms of money will necessarily be positive. Assuming a positive rate of interest in a setting designed to shed light on the reasons for a positive rate of interest is, moreover, clearly of particularly dubious value.

We thus conclude as follows: MISES does go beyond FETTER in explicitly attempting to explain why the rate of interest in competitive economies is generally greater than zero. His attempt to do so in a purely subjective theory, however, is unsuccessful. MISES' failure is due in part to a confused notion of time preference. Like FETTER, MISES does not address the further question of the determination of the size of the rate of interest, his analysis of the phenomenon of interest thus remaining in this respect inferior in scope to BÖHM-BAWERK's. The remainder of his positive contribution to the explanation of the phenomenon of interest does not go anywhere beyond that contained in BÖHM-BAWERK's *Positive Theory*.

---

83 Fish paradoxically being the perishable good par excellence, MISES' concept of time preference is not applicable, for instance, to BÖHM-BAWERK's boat and net example.

This is particularly true of his theory of distribution and his conclusions for the social problem of interest (cf. 1949: 521).

Chapter 6

Murray N. ROTHBARD's Development of the MISESian "Pure Time Preference Theory of Interest"

Murray N. ROTHBARD's main contribution to the theory of interest is also to be found in his fundamental work, entitled *Man, Economy, and State* (1962). Since the renaissance of Austrian subjectivism in the seventies, however, he has made a number of further contributions to the subject, foremost among them the "Introduction" to his edition of FETTER's essays on *Capital, Interest, and Rent* (1977a),[84] and his article on "Time Preference" in the *New Palgrave Dictionary of Economics* (1987; cf.1987a, 1987b).

ROTHBARD fully embraces MISES' development of the pure time preference theory, which he attempts to extend, as we shall see, into an explanation of the *determination of the size* of the rate of interest. ROTHBARD identifies "the *locus classicus* of the time preference theory of interest" (1987: 645; cf. 1962: 332n12) in BÖHM-BAWERK's *Capital and Interest*. FETTER, "building on Böhm-Bawerk, completely discarded productivity as an explanation of interest and constructed an integrated theory of distribution in which interest is *determined* solely by time preference" (1987: 645, e.a.; cf. 1987a: 308, 1977a: 4, 1962: 332n12). MISES is hailed for his "adoption" (1987: 646) and "resurrection of Fetter's pure time preference theory of interest" (1987b: 480; cf. 1962: 332n12) and for his correction of "Fetter's only mistake in interest theory" which "was to deny FISHER's assertion that time preference (or, as FISHER called it, 'impatience') is a universal and *necessary* fact of human action. For a demonstration of this important truth, see MISES (1949: 480ff)" (1962: 364n27):

> "Mises made clear that a positive time preference rate is an essential attribute of human nature. Secondly, and as a corollary, whereas Fetter believed that people could have either positive or negative rates of time preference, Mises demonstrated that a positive rate is deducible from the fact of human action ... ." (1987: 646)

ROTHBARD is the only pure time preference theorist who provides what must be regarded as a *definition* of the concept of time preference, although surprisingly this definition is relegated only to a footnote. Instead of focusing on one particular meaning of time preference, however, his definition contains a multitude of meanings *all at once*:

---

84 For an enthusiastic review of this "Introduction," which has become a regular part of the reading requirements for Austrian Economics Seminar sessions dealing with the theory of capital and interest (cf. also LITTLECHILD ed. 1990, II: 108-30), see Kirzner (1980).

> "*Time preference* may be called the preference for *present satisfaction* over *future satisfaction* or *present good* over *future good*, provided it is remembered that it is the *same* satisfaction (or 'good') that is being compared over the periods of time." (1962: 13n15)

A lot depends, of course, on the meaning attached to the predicate "same." Indeed, ROTHBARD immediately proceeds to clarify this meaning in dealing with the notorious ice-in-winter/ice-in-summer counterexample:

> "Thus, a common type of objection to the assertion of universal time preference is that, in the winter time, a man will prefer the delivery of ice the next summer (future) to delivery of ice in the present. This, however, confuses the concept 'good' with the material properties of a thing, whereas it actually refers to subjective satisfactions. Since ice-in-the-summer provides different (and greater) satisfactions that ice-in-the-winter, they are *not* the same but *different* goods. In this case, it is different satisfactions that are being compared, despite the fact that the *physical* property of the thing may be the same." (1962: 13n15)

Note that where MISES had employed an objectivist, backward-looking, production-oriented criterion for determining "sameness," ROTHBARD uses a characteristically subjectivist, forward-looking criterion. It is left unclear, however, whether this criterion is to determine "sameness" only with respect to quality, thus leaving "sameness" of quantity to be determined by an objective criterion, or whether it is to determine "sameness" also with respect to quantity. But even disregarding this problem, no unequivocal definition of time preference emerges. Thus we are left with a definition in terms of present goods and "same" future goods, with "sameness," in the sense of "providing a satisfaction considered of equal importance except for the time dimension," presumably to be ascertained by the agent making the intertemporal choice. How this agent is to separate his judgement with respect to "sameness" from that with respect to time preference is left entirely unclear. ROTHBARD thus effectively carries the difficulties encountered in the context of a definition of time preference in terms of satisfactions over to the definition of time preference in terms of goods. Considering that ROTHBARD later characterizes money as "clearly the present good *par excellence*" and future goods as "*present expectations of the future acquisition of money*" (1962: 320; cf. 298), his definition also encompasses time preference in terms of money. It is again restricted, however, to situations where present and future money (presumably equal amounts) confer equal satisfaction - with all resultant problems concerning the separation of the two decisions involved. Finally, the passage contains the definition in terms of present and "same" future satisfaction, with "same" meaning "considered subjectively of equal importance."

Indeed, we find ROTHBARD expressing time preference in all three of these senses throughout his reasoning on interest, although no further mention is made of any of the finer points concerning the determination of "sameness." Thus, we find time preference severally expressed in terms of goods (1962: 298, 300-1,

318-20); and yet we are puzzled by the fact that "the premium of a given good at present over the present *prospect* of its *future* acquisition" is characterized as the *result* of "the universal fact of time preference," rather than as an instance of time preference *itself* (1962: 320). ROTHBARD also expresses time preference severally in terms of money (1962: 320, 326, 330); but again he says that "it follows from the law of time preference that *present money is worth more than present expectations of the future acquisition of money*" (1962: 320), alluding thus again to some deeper meaning attached to the notion of time preference.[85] Finally, he also expresses time preference in terms of satisfaction (1962: 318; cf. 13, 273-4); but once more it is said to be "because of the universal fact of time preference" that "future satisfaction is always at a discount compared to present satisfaction" (1962: 318).

In order to find out more about a possible deeper meaning ROTHBARD attaches to the notion of time preference, we look to his proof of "the universal fact of time preference." ROTHBARD expounds this proof in the following passage:

> "A fundamental and constant truth about human nature is that *man prefers his end to be achieved in the shortest possible time*. Given the specific satisfaction, the sooner it arrives, the better. This results from the fact that time is always scarce, and a means to be economized. The sooner any end is attained, the better. Thus, with any *given end* to be attained, the shorter the period of action, i.e., production, the more preferable for the actor. *This is the universal fact of time preference*." (1962: 13; cf. passim)

As a proof, however, this is rather cryptic; for neither is it clear what is meant by "the fact that time is always scarce" nor are we told *how* "the universal fact of time preference" is to result from this scarcity. In another passage we read:

> "Every person prefers and will attempt to achieve the satisfaction of a given end in the present to the satisfaction of that end in the future. This is the law of time preference." (1962: 273-4)

But again this is not a proof, but rather an assertion of a "law of time preference." In addition, both passages appear to involve a concept of time preference that differs from all three of those implied in ROTHBARD's definition; for time preference is now employed in the sense of the preference for the achievement of a given present satisfaction in the present over the achievement of the *same identical present* satisfaction in the future (such as the preference for quenching present thirst in the present over quenching the same present thirst in the future; cf. Chapter 3 above). It is indeed in this peculiar sense that ROTHBARD seems to credit MISES with having "demonstrated" the universality of the "law of time preference:"

---

[85] And yet, ROTHBARD's recent contribution to *The New Palgrave* regarding the concept of "time preference" contains the following definition: "Time preference is the insight that people prefer 'present goods' (goods available for use at present) to 'future goods' (present expectations of goods becoming available at some date in the future) ... ." (1987: 644)

> "... Mises demonstrated that a positive rate (of time preference, I.P.) is deducible from the fact of human action, since by the very nature of a goal or an end people wish to achieve that goal as soon as possible." (1987: 646)

We note that, rather than being a faithful rendering of the argument presented by MISES, this is a special interpretation of that argument (cf. Chapter 5 above). For MISES' position, viz., that the very fact that agents do act (instead of deferring action) implies that earlier satisfaction is preferred over later satisfaction, left it open whether the actions compared are directed at the gratification of different (but related) desires, or at the gratification of one and the same desire. ROTHBARD implicitly opts for the latter interpretation. No indication is given, however, of the relation of time preference in *this* sense to the phenomenon of interest, or of how time preference in *this* sense carries over to time preference in terms of "goods" or "money." Thus, ROTHBARD has no more provided a satisfactory explanation of the general positivity of the sign of the rate of interest than have either FETTER or MISES.

ROTHBARD goes on to demonstrate (1962: ch.6) that even the size of the interest rate is "determined solely by the time preferences of the individuals in the society, and by no other factor" (1962: 332). He thus extends the scope of the pure time preference theory beyond that (implicitly) accorded it by FETTER and MISES - although we note that ROTHBARD may not have been aware of this since he credits both his predecessors with having already presented theories of interest rate *determination* (1987: 644, 645; 1962: 332n12). ROTHBARD develops his argument in the context of a money economy, expressing time preference in terms of money throughout and stressing its marginal nature: for "as present money dwindels and future money increases in a man's possession, the marginal utility of the former increases on the man's value scale, and the marginal utility of the latter decreases" (1962: 329-30; cf. 324, 380, 1977a: 4, 17-8). This does not seem to impair (as it easily could), however, the operation of "the law of time preference," i.e., the fact that time preference is always in favor of the present (1962: 326, 330). For each individual there is thus a critical *positive* rate of interest at which he will neither supply nor demand present money in exchange for future money. With the interest rate increasing above this critical rate, the individual will exhibit a monotonously increasing *supply* of present in exchange for future money, whereas with the interest rate decreasing below the critical rate he will exhibit a monotonously increasing *demand* for present in exchange for future money (1962: 324-31). Horizontal aggregation of individual schedules will yield an upward-sloping aggregate supply and a downward-sloping aggregate demand curve, the intersection of which will determine the equilibrium market rate of interest (1962: 331-2). Thus ROTHBARD concludes that

> "... once again, it is utilities and utilities alone, here in the form of time preferences, that determine the market result; the explanation does not lie in some sort of 'mutually determining process' ... ." (1962: 326; cf. 323, 332)

In particular, even a fivefold increase in the physical productivity of factors of production, so ROTHBARD, would in the long run tend to so affect both factor and product prices that the rate of interest, the price spread between product and aggregate factor prices, would ultimately remain unchanged (1962: 362-3):

> "Thus the productivity of production processes has no basic relation to the rate of return on business investment. This rate of return depends on the price spreads between stages, and these price spreads will tend to be equal. The size of the price spread, i.e., the size of the interest rate, is determined, as we have seen at length, by the time-preference schedules of all the individuals in the economy." (1962: 363)[86]

ROTHBARD does acknowledge, however, the effect on the rate of interest of other "factors affecting time preferences," among which he lists the psychological framework, life expectancy, and real money stock of the individuals in the economy (1962: 380-1). But whereas psychological framework and life expectancy may perhaps indeed be legitimately regarded as counting among those factors that "must be taken, in the final analysis, as data by economists" (1962: 380), the real money stock is surely of a different caliber. It is undoubtedly itself one of the central endogenous variables of an economy. ROTHBARD has not shown, for instance, that a change in the physical productivity conditions does not affect the real money stock of the individuals in the economy, and thus their individual schedules and the rate of interest. His analysis of the determination of the size of the rate of interest is thus incomplete, at best, and his conclusion with respect to the *sole* importance of time preference inadequately founded.[87]

Once again we have thus not discovered a satisfactory *positive* theory of interest. ROTHBARD's analysis of the reasons for the general positivity of the sign of the rate of interest was seen to suffer from several confusions in the definition of time preference itself: Not only did the notion of time preference itself remain ambiguous; more importantly, conclusions drawn with respect to one notion of time preference (defined in terms of one and the same satisfaction, or goal, attained in the nearer or remoter future) were transferred without further ado to others (notions of time preference defined in terms goods or money). ROTHBARD's conclusion with respect to the sole importance of individual time preference schedules in determining the size of the rate of interest were seen to be inade-

---

86 More recently - and inconsistently with this analysis - ROTHBARD (1977a: 15-6) has seemed rather to support FETTER's contention that a rise in physical productivity would tend to lower the rate of interest (1914: 247) - a contention that we have found equally unfounded, however (cf. Chapter 4).

87 As we shall see in Chapter 9 below, ROTHBARD's explanation is fundamentally identical to FISHER's first approximation.

quately founded insofar as the effect, for instance, of physical productivity conditions on the real money stock of these individuals was not considered. Once more we must conclude that what remains of a positive analysis of the interest problem does not go beyond the insights attained by BÖHM-BAWERK, and outlined in Chapter 2 of the present investigation. As in the case of FETTER and MISES, the same is true of ROTHBARD's conclusions for the theory of distribution and the social problem of interest.

Chapter 7

More Recent Offerings of the Pure Time Preference Theory of Interest

FETTER, MISES, and ROTHBARD are the only pure time preference theorists who have provided what may be considered full-scale expositions of that theory. Since the renaissance of Austrian economics in the mid-seventies, however, there has appeared a number of contributions defending, explicating, or interpreting that theory (O'DRISCOLL 1979; cf. 1980; GARRISON 1979, 1979a, 1988; cf. 1985; KIRZNER 1976, 1983, 1986, cf. 1980, 1983a). As noted in the Introduction, the pure time preference theory has also found its way into at least one American mid-level microeconomics textbook (BAIRD 1982). In the present Chapter, we shall briefly evaluate these contributions, again with a view to the central theme pursued in this investigation.

7.1 Gerald P. O'DRISCOLL

In a paper entitled "The Time Preference Theory of Interest Rate Determination" (1979),[88] O'DRISCOLL emphatically interprets that theory as encompassing both an explanation of the general positivity of the *sign* (1979: 21) and, as the title of his paper indicates, an explanation of the *determination* of the *size* of the rate of interest (1979: 1, 11, 19, 21, 30).[89] Since in the pure time preference theory "time preference alone *determines* the long run equilibrium real interest rate," whereas "in Fisher's theory productivity elements and time preference jointly *determine* the long run equilibrium real rate," O'DRISCOLL diagnoses a "contradiction" (1979: 11, e.a.; cf. 1) with modern BÖHM-FISHER-based time-preference-cum-productivity explanations of interest rate determination, as epitomized in the Fisher-diagram (cf. 1979: 4-5, 35). He proposes that

---

[88] Elsewhere in his paper, O'DRISCOLL also refers to the *pure* time preference theory (e.g. 1979: 4, 11).

[89] O'DRISCOLL is primarily concerned with an exposition of FETTER's contribution (cf. 1979: 1-3, and passim), which he says has been "adopted" by MISES and ROTHBARD (1979: 38, 39). He does not detail FETTER's (or any other) explanation of why time preference is in favor of the present and thus why the rate of interest is generally positive, however, and there is only a general footnote reference (1979: 30n44) to ROTHBARD's *determination* of the size of the rate of interest, intended to support the contention that "Fetter's pure time preference theory can be as readily translated into demand and supply analysis as can Fisher's" (1979: 30). We are not told, however, how FISHER's theory can be (or where it is) thus translated.

> "(s)olution of this contradiction involves the recognition of two different conceptions of 'time preference,' reinforced by two different conceptualizations of the interest problem." (1979: 11)[90]

With respect to the concept of time preference, O'DRISCOLL argues that whereas modern theorists employ a marginal definition of time preference, gauged with reference to some arbitrary benchmark such as a uniform pattern of consumption over time,[91] "Fetter and later pure time preference theorists (as well as Böhm-Bawerk) adopted a non-marginal definition of time preference" (1979: 9). This is described as follows:

> "... (T)here is time preference in Fetter's sense whenever the present value of a future service is less than its future value. In the time preference view put forth by Fetter ... (i)f a net return on investing is being earned, there is time discounting, which is what the pure time preference theorists have meant by time preference." (1979: 23)

But, as far as O'DRISCOLL's definition of time preference is intelligible at all,[92] it does not characterize a non-marginal as opposed to a marginal,[93] but rather an endogenous as opposed to an exogenous conception of time preference.[94] Indeed, we have seen all pure time preference theorists (including BÖHM-BAWERK and FISHER) to have employed endogenous (but often marginal) concepts of time preference. We note, however, that an endogenization of the concept of time preference does not *in and of itself* impair the alleged use of the FISHER-diagram in exemplifying the role of technological considerations in co-determining at what margin the rate of time preference will settle.

---

90 Considering O'DRISCOLL's assertions that FETTER's critique of FISHER showed that "Fisher committed a logical error and that Fisherians are perpetuating it" (1979: 7), that "no logical defense against Fetter's critique existed" (1979: 33), that "the Fisherian system is thus formally deficient and incapable of determining the equilibrium rate of interest" (1979: 33), and finally that therefore "Fetter's theory is 'annihilatory' of Fisher's" (1979: 34), it may come as a surprise that any further contradiction should need solving. In fact, in confronting FETTER's and FISHER's explanations of interest rate determination, O'DRISCOLL implicitly pursues *two* objectives: one is to present FETTER's critique of FISHER; the other is to show that FETTER's underlying conception of an explanation of interest rate determination differed from FISHER's. Since we wish to evaluate only the *positive* elements of the pure time preference theory, we are exclusively concerned with the latter.

91 As already mentioned, O'DRISCOLL (1979: 9n6) mistakenly ascribes such concept to FISHER (1930: 61-8).

92 It seems to be of dubious use to define (positive) time preference, as O'DRISCOLL does, in terms of the very phenomenon (positive) time preference is supposed to explain, i.e., the existence of originary interest.

93 Surely, the inference that some utility is apparently derived from a good for which a positive price is being paid does not imply that utility is a nonmarginal concept. This reasoning is analogous, however, to O'DRISCOLL's.

94 O'DRISCOLL seems implicitly to define time preference in terms of goods, or rather services of goods, of equal quantity and quality. We are not here concerned with this aspect of his definition, however, and neither is he.

We thus turn to consider said "reinforcement" of the time preference theorists' definition of time preference by a different conceptualization of the interest problem. This apparently[95] involves a reaffirmation of the distinction - drawn by BÖHM-BAWERK (cf. Chapter 2), but rejected by FISHER (cf. Chapter 3) and later theorists[96] - between an explanation of the positivity of the *sign* and an explanation of the determination of the *size* of the rate of interest (1979: 20-1).[97] The former, according to O'DRISCOLL, provides insights that are a necessary prerequisite for the latter:

> "For Fetter, answering the question of the nature and necessity of a positive interest rate provided the assumptions necessary for determining at what (positive) level the rate would settle ... ." (1979: 21)[98]

Since he repeatedly states that FETTER (and his followers) were not questioning the technique of mutul determination (1979: 19, 21), O'DRISCOLL seems to be saying that the explanation of the "nature and necessity" of interest - identified with an explanation of the positivity of the sign of the rate of interest, assumed to be furnishable by time preference alone - establishes some sort of "causal priority" for time preference over technology in the determination of the rate of interest. It is presumably thus that O'DRISCOLL (1979: 31) can approvingly quote FETTER's acknowledgement of the effect a change in productivity conditions would have on the rate of interest without being deterred from adherence to a pure time preference theory of interest rate *determination*:

> "Productivity is not an independent variable in interest rate determination, as in the Fisherian paradigm; its effect on interest rates is only indirect, via induced changes in time preference. In other words, technical productivity might be an argument in the 'psychological function' determining time preference, but it is not a codeterminant (together with time preference) of interest rates." (1979: 31-2)

This echoes FETTER's view (cf. Chapter 4 above) - although FETTER never extended it into an *explicit* proposition about interest rate *determination* by time preference alone. It is clear that such extension implies a concept of "determination" that differs fundamentally from the one implicitly used so far in this investigation. We can readily see how an exogenous concept of time prefer-

---

95 Since it is not entirely clear in O'DRISCOLL's paper what he means by "a different conceptualization of the interest problem," the following is an interpretation. - O'DRISCOLL also laments, for instance, the influence exercized on later real theories of interest by the FISHER-diagram (1979: 4-5); but he calls this "Fisher's *formulation* of the problem," and goes on to add that "they (later real theories of interest, I.P.) are *also* governed by his *conceptualization* of the problem" (1979: 5, e.a.; cf. 7).

96 Cf. e.g. LUTZ (1967: 10). For a counterexample, see FABER (1979).

97 I have not been able to ascertain O'DRISCOLL's (1979: 20-1) unsubstantiated attribution of this reaffirmation to FETTER.

98 The reader is reminded that in the view proposed in the present investigation, FETTER provided *no* satisfactory explanation of the general positivity of the rate of interest at all. Much less did he provide a systematic investigation of the forces determining "at what level the rate would settle."

ence may be considered irrelevant in the context of such "conceptualization of the interest problem." And it is against the background of such conceptualization that we must interpret O'DRISCOLL's surprising dictum that

> "to a pure time preference theorist, once one understands time preference in a nonmarginal or absolute[99] sense, one has explained fully the determination of equilibrium interest rates" (1979: 9).

We note, however, that it is not clear *how* causal priority of time preference over productivity considerations in the determination of the rate of interest is established through a demonstration of its "nature and necessity," i.e., through an explanation of why the rate of interest is generally positive. Moreover, in the view proposed in this investigation none of the pure time preference theorists succeeded in providing a satisfactory explanation of the general positivity of the rate of interest, and FETTER can hardly be said to have provided any such explanation at all. O'DRISCOLL's considerations thus do not detract from the negative conclusions reached so far with respect to the positive elements contained in the pure time preference theory of interest.

7.2 Roger W. GARRISON

GARRISON is also much concerned with clarifying the "fundamental difference" (1979: 144) between the neoclassical and the MISESian concept of time preference: whereas the former is "expressed in terms of some homogeneous consumption good" and gauged with reference to a uniform pattern of consumption over time (1979: 142-3), the latter "was formulated not in terms of consumption goods and patterns of consumption, but rather in terms of *action*" (1979: 143). But GARRISON merely proceeds to paraphrase MISES' "praxeological" proof of the universal validity of (positive) time preference (1979: 143-4) instead of providing us with a much needed clarification of the concept of time preference contained therein. Accordingly, the definitions given or implied in GARRISON's contributions are themselves characteristically vague and ambiguous;[100] they include, we note, the definition of time preference implied in ROTHBARD's peculiar version of MISES' proof of the universal validity of time preference, i.e., the "general prefer-

---

99 Meaning, in our interpretation: endogenous.

100 We find definitions, for instance, in terms of "a preference for *consumption* in the nearer future to consumption in the more remote future" (1979: 143, e.a.), "a preference for *acquiring these goods* at an earlier point in the future over acquiring them at a more remote point in the future" (1979: 144, e.a.), "a systematic preference for *sooner rather than later*" (1985: 169, e.a.),"the systematic *discounting of the future*" (1985: 169, 1988: 45, e.a.), "the general preference ... for *output* sooner over *output* later" (1988: 47, e.a.), or "the general preference for achieving *ends* sooner over achieving them later" (1988: 48, e.a.).

ence for achieving ends sooner over achieving them later" (1988: 48). GARRISON adds a curious touch to pure time preference theorists' explanations of the general positivity of the rate of interest in his reply to STIGLER's assertion that the rate of interest reckoned in terms of a commodity that is not costlessly storable (because of the possibility of theft or accidental destruction, for instance) might conceivably be negative (1966: 278):[101]

> "In transactions of this sort the individual 'lender' is, from his own perspective, purchasing theft-prevention or accident prevention services. The payment for these preventative services must be kept conceptually distinct from the payment of interest." (1979: 147)

GARRISON thus wants to counter the impression, created by "neoclassical interest theory," that the assumptions of costless storage (and non-perishability[102]) "are necessary to preclude the possibility of a negative rate of interest" (1979: 147).[103] But with a time preference theorem thus restricted to goods that are costlessly storable (and non-perishable), what need is there for any "praxeological proof" of the fact that there will never be a preference for future over present goods? Moreover, how can a time preference theorem thus restricted be applied to explain a phenomenon that arises in intertemporal exchanges in terms of goods, such as money, that are characteristically *not* costlessly storable? GARRISON's reply to STIGLER thus implies an abandonment of the attempt to explain the *real* world phenomenon of interest.

GARRISON is somewhat more reluctant than O'DRISCOLL to designate the time preference theory as a theory of interest rate *determination*,[104] and he is careful to avoid the predicate "pure" - possibly lest it should be associated with the proposition that a change in productivity conditions would have no effect at all upon the rate of interest. Indeed, in response to YEAGER's assertion that a general increase in physical productivity would cause the interest rate to rise (1979: 208), GARRISON contends that the interest rate may rather rise *or fall*, and he lends

---

101 We are reminded of STIGLER's related criticism of BÖHM-BAWERK's proposition, offered in the context of his first cause, that a unit of present money will always be preferred over a unit of future money (cf. Chapter 2 above).

102 Both STIGLER's argument and GARRISON's counterargument equally apply to the case of non-perishability.

103 The reader is reminded of MISES' and ROTHBARD's quite different arguments offered in dealing with the ice-in-winter/ice-in-summer counterexample to the "universal" preference for present over future goods.

104 This reluctance is plainly transparent in the last phrase of the following passage in which GARRISON contrasts the time preference theory with time preference cum productivity explanations of interest: "Are time preferences of market participants and capital productivity independent co-*determinants of the rate of interest*, as Irving Fisher would have it? Or does time preference alone - the systematic discounting of the future - *account for the payment that we call interest*?" (1988: 45, e.a.)

support to the proposition (falsely ascribed to FETTER instead of FISHER, cf. Chapter 4 above)[105] that the rise in physical productivity leads to an increase in wealth, and that, "*to the extent that* increased wealth is associated with a fall in time preference, a lower rate of discount and a lower rate of interest would result" (1979a: 221, e.a.[106]). But GARRISON seems to have no qualms with ROTHBARD's determination of the rate of interest by time preference alone (1979a: 220n29; cf. 1988: 53, and passim); and again and again, he contrasts the time preference theory favorably with other theories of interest rate *determination* (1979: 146, 1988: 49, 52), thus intimating that it is in some sense a competitor in this particular scientific endeavor. In GARRISON's case, unfortunately, this sense is never clearly specified.

7.3 Charles W. BAIRD

BAIRD defines time preference both in terms of money (1982: 302) and in terms of consumption goods (1982: 304); in both cases he explicitly emphasizes the marginal character of the concept, i.e., the dependence of the rate of time preference on the intertemporal distribution of money or goods respectively (1982: 303, 304). In a section entitled "Why Interest Rates are Positive" he attempts to prove the general positivity of time preference, however, *whatever* the intertemporal distribution. But he ends up supplying not one, but two proofs. The first is couched in terms of money:

> "By giving up a dollar today in exchange for a dollar next year you are giving up the ability to purchase goods during *this* year, and next year's dollar cannot restore that ability. You are postponing the enjoyment of what you could buy with a dollar, and you are receiving nothing for the sacrifice. Most people would insist on some reward for giving up the *current use* of their purchasing power. In other words, they would be willing to give up less than a dollar today in exchange for a dollar next year." (1982: 301-2)

This proof presupposes, however, that the enjoyment that could be had from that money today is greater than the enjoyment that could be had from that money next year, and that has by no means been proven. The second proof is also couched in terms of money. BAIRD here argues that, even if "you receive a large income this year but face zero income receipts next year" so that you would leave some of your present income unused

> "... you wouldn't lend the money to anyone else unless you received a positive interest rate (even with no risk of default), because when someone else has it you loose the option to use it in the current year. You couldn't, in other

[105] The priority, in any case, is clearly FISHER's.

[106] We note that the caution, however, is GARRISON's.

> words, change your mind halfway through the year and use the money then. That option has a positive value." (1982: 302)[107]

This argument (which implies an uncertain future) will be recognized to be identical with the argument offered by BÖHM-BAWERK in the context of his first cause, so that STIGLER's stricture (cf. Chapter 2 above) equally applies: money not being costlessly storable, present money may well be exchanged for a lesser amount of future money, even with BAIRD's option having a positive value. We may, of course, try GARRISON's way out and deny that this is a case of "pure" intertemporal exchange at all since the lender is buying not only future money but storage services also. But we have already noted the impasse this leaves us in.

BAIRD seems to be reluctant to interpret the time preference theory also as a theory of interest rate *determination*; but he asserts that "interest rates are the result of the interplay between the marginal time preference rates of borrowers and lenders" (1982: 303).[108] In a section entitled "The Primacy of Time Preference," BAIRD does note that "the physical productivity of current capital goods will affect interest rates" (1982: 304); but he cautions that

> "(p)hysical productivity of capital goods is not an independent influence on interest rates; rather, its effect on interest rates works through its effect on marginal rates of time preference" (1982: 304),

thereby implicitly following FETTER and O'DRISCOLL in suggesting some sort of causal predominance for time preference in the *determination* of the rate of interest. But, like FETTER (and unlike O'DRSICOLL), BAIRD merely asserts this position, instead of consistently arguing it.

7.4 Israel M. KIRZNER

An interesting "Attempt at Clarification" of "The Pure Time Preference Theory of Interest" has recently been offered by KIRZNER (1993). KIRZNER invokes BÖHM-BAWERK's defense, in response to FISHER's criticism,[109] of the distinction

---

107 It is not clear why BAIRD cautiously restricts both his arguments to "most people" (1982: 302). Since it is tacitly implied that if "most people" prefer present money to future, the rate of interest will be positive, "most" in this context is obviously to be interpreted in the sense of "a number sufficient for a positive interest rate to result."

108 Note BAIRD's uncertainty in dealing with the fact that borrowers of funds for productive purposes are guided by the rates of return on these funds obtainable in the market. These rates of return, BAIRD explains, exist "precisely because, *and perhaps only because*, people insist on a bribe to give up current availability of purchasing power. The measured positive rate of return ... *could well be* simply a result of the fact that most people have positive (and declining) marginal time preference rates ... ." (1982: 303, emphases altered).

109 FISHER's position is cited in a preceding note to the present chapter. FISHER later reaffirms his position (1930: 13-4), without as much as mentioning BÖHM-BAWERK's response.

between the question why the rate of interest is generally positive and how the rate of interest is determined (1993: 183-4). BÖHM-BAWERK argues that

> "all interest-originating causes are also determining factors for the actual rate. But not all rate-determining factors are also interest-creating causes. ... When we enquire into the causes of a flood we certainly cannot cite the dams and reservoirs built to prevent or at least mitigate inundations. But they are a determining factor for the actual water-mark of the flood. ... Similarly there are other circumstances besides the actual interest-creating causes that bring about or enhance the value advantage of present goods over future goods." (III: 192,[110] cited in KIRZNER 1993: 183-4)

KIRZNER significantly reaffirms BÖHM-BAWERK's distinction between "originating causes" and "determining factors," arguing that the problem as originally posed by BÖHM-BAWERK - the explanation of the general existence of originary interest and its corollary, the existence of laborless income (KIRZNER 1993: 179-80; cf. Chapter 2 above) - requires a search for the originating causes rather than the determining factors of the phenomenon in question. He identifies *one* "source of modern bewilderment" (1993: 182) with the pure time preference theory in the very fact that it has been misinterpreted as a theory of the determination of the size of the rate of interest.[111] KIRZNER regrets that such misinterpretation has been nourished by the fact that

> "(a)dmittedly, some expositions of PTPT[112] have sometimes unfortunately permitted it to be thought that, since only time preference accounts for the *existence* of interest, it follows that a change in the conditions of physical productivity would invariably leave the the rate of interest unchanged.[113] But in fact PTPT implies nothing of the kind.[114] ... PTPT theorists do recognize that since the prevalence of positive time preference does generate the phenomenon of interest, it cannot at all be ruled out that other factors (including physical productivity) may effect the determination of its rate. For example, physical productivity may significantly affect the level of wealth, and thus the marginal rate of time preference.[115] All PTPT insists on is that, no matter how

110 In the original, BÖHM-BAWERK differentiates between "Entstehungs*gründen*" and "Bestimm*gründen*" in the former part of the statement, and (somewhat inconsistently) between "Entstehungs*ursachen*" and "Bestimm*gründen*" in the latter. In the translation here rendered, SENNHOLZ has kept to a translation of the latter terminology ("originating *causes*" and "determining *factors*") throughout. KIRZNER differentiates between "originating *factors*" and "determining *factors*." In order to avoid terminological confusion, we keep to SENNHOLZ's terminology.

111 KIRZNER identifies another source of modern bewilderment with the pure time preference theory in "an implicit denial (in modern interest theory, I.P.) of the value-productivity phenomenon seen as calling for explanation in Böhm-Bawerk's view (and in PTPT's view)" (1993: 182). "PTPT" is KIRZNER's abbreviation of "pure time preference theory (of interest)" (1993: 166).

112 Cf. the preceding footnote.

113 KIRZNER provides no references. Note that at least one expositor has not only "permitted it to be thought" but has said so *explicitly*.

114 There is a footnote reference at this point to FETTER (1914: 247; cf. Chapter 4 above) who "was quite explicit on this point" (1993: 185n25).

115 Note the change in emphasis: Whereas FETTER (seconded by O'DRISCOLL) argued (inconclusively) that an increase in physical productivity would be followed by an increase

> significant a role physical productivity may play among the complete list of variables affecting the rate of interest, it is fallacious to refer to interest income ... as the fruit of the physical productivity of agents of production." (1993: 186)

KIRZNER then proceeds to show how this "essentialist" interpretation of the pure time preference theory fits in with the "methodological essentialism" Austrian subjectivists since MENGER have traditionally espoused (1993: 186-8). KIRZNER thus follows BÖHM-BAWERK in identifying an explanation of the *positivity* of the rate of interest with an isolation of the *originating causes* of interest which he then identifies in its turn with providing an insight into the "essence" or "nature" of interest. We shall deal with these propositions in more detail in the subsequent chapter.

A more ostensible problem, in the context of the present investigation, with KIRZNER's "Attempt at Clarification" lies in the fact that he identifies the pure time preference theory with an alternative explanation of the *positivity* of the rate of interest. According to KIRZNER, the pure time preference theory explains this phenomenon "by appeal to widespread, possibly universal, positive time preference" (1993: 171; cf. 192); time preference is positive because "people do prefer, other aspects of the situation aside, to achieve their goals sooner rather than later" (1993: 172; cf. 178, 192).[116] This clearly coincides with ROTHBARD's interpretation of the MISESian argument in support of the universal validity of positive time preference. But, as was argued above, this reasoning presupposes that people evaluate present and future means to the attainment of their goals with reference to the same identical present goal - a presupposition that, we argued, is entirely unwarranted. If people are free to valuate present and future goods each with respect to the satisfaction of whichever want they believe most important, there is no a priori reason why future goods should not be preferred over present goods.

---

in the provision for the present and a resultant decrease in the rate of time preference, and GARRISON asserted that the rate of time preference would fall *if* wealth increased, KIRZNER does no longer offer even a conditional prediction concerning the effect of a productivity increase on the rate of time preference (and, by implication, on the rate of interest).

116 It is not clear why with time preference *thus defined*, the positivity of time preference should be merely "widespread" and only *possibly* "universal." Nor is it clear (at least not without further argument) how, with positive time preference only *widespread*, the rate of interest will necessarily be positive. This might depend, for example, on the relative buying power of those with and those without positive time preference.

Chapter 8

The Pure Time Preference Theory of Interest: A Reevaluation

KIRZNER's "Attempt at Clarification" thus fails because pure time preference theorists have not only offered no satisfactory explanation of the determination of the size of the rate of interest; according to our investigation, they have not offered a satisfactory explanation of why time preference, and thus the rate of interest, is generally positive. Although this charge is perhaps here consistently argued for the first time, its theme should not be so entirely new to pure time preference theorists. Thus, in criticizing MISES' time preference theory, KNIGHT proclaimed his belief

> "... that apart from the productivity of investment no assertion could be made about time preference - correctly defined[117] - as a human trait." (KNIGHT 1941: 412)

Three decades earlier, SEAGER had already argued in somewhat similar fashion against the "purely psychological" theory of interest (identified by him - with not unquestionable justification, as we shall see in the Appendix - primarily with FISHER's "impatience theory of interest") that,

> "(s)o far as I can see, with the technical superiority of present over future goods, or the productivity of capital, absent, the question as to whether interest would continue or not is an entirely open one." (SEAGER 1912: 841)

Both SEAGER and KNIGHT were arguing, of course, on the basis of their own productivity theories of interest. One may, however, perhaps agree with their indictments *without necessarily* being compelled to a view that sees interest as the reward for the productive services of a factor of production. After all, BÖHM-BAWERK himself, as we saw, accorded *some* role to productivity in the explanation of the positivity of the rate of interest without at the same time seeing interest as "essentially" a productivity return. The same is true of FISHER, as we shall see in detail below. In order to explain all this, we shall now proceed to suggest a reinterpretation of BÖHM-BAWERK's *Positive Theory* which will entail a corresponding reinterpretation of the pure time preference theory of interest.

Why it is that in competitive economies there is generally a difference between the value of a factor of production and the value of the product attributed

[117] The definition suggested by KNIGHT as being "correct" is what has above (Chapter 3) been called the "neoclassical" definition of time preference: "As to the meaning of time preference," Knight writes, "a real and meaningful preference of present over future would be manifested in behaviour by a choice of a higher rate of enjoyment now and a lower rate in the future, over a uniform rate, *ceteris paribus*, i.e., the total being given and freedom allowed as to the distribution in time." (1941: 412-3)

to its assistance? Why does competition not erode this difference? In asking this question, BÖHM-BAWERK was indeed "seeking an explanation for an observed phenomenon which is, in the absence of a theory of interest, unable to be accounted for" (KIRZNER 1993: 168). *This* question is *fully* answered, however, once one has pointed out that production takes time and that the time dimension of goods matters as naturally, if not as obviously, for their valuation as do their physical and space dimensions. Competition does erode all value difference - over and above that duly and faithfully reflecting the time dimension of the goods and services considered. The problem with the exposition in the *Positive Theory* is that BÖHM-BAWERK immediately mingles this problem of the explanation of the mere *existence* of a rate of interest with the *further* problem of the explanation of the general positivity of that rate, and proceeds to treat both questions together under the heading of "The Origin of Interest." We have seen, and we can readily understand, why he did so: BÖHM-BAWERK wanted to explain the existence of laborless income in competitive "capitalist" economies. "*Whence and why*," we have quoted him formulating "the problem of interest" at the outset, "*does the capitalist receive this endless and effortless flow of wealth?*" The reception of laborless income in capitalist societies did and does indeed generally go hand in hand with the existence of a positive rate of interest. BÖHM-BAWERK thus naturally combines the question of the mere *existence* of a rate of interest (negative or positive) with the further question of its general positivity, and answers both before drawing any conclusions regarding the nature or essence of interest, the theory of distribution, or the social problem of interest. But we saw that the conclusions he draws are quite independent of the reasons given for the general positivity of the rate of interest. This is taken as indirect support of our contention that the aspect here emphasized is indeed an *independent* aspect of BÖHM-BAWERK's *Positive Theory* - one that, moreover, has been regarded by SCHUMPETER as "perhaps the most important of all" (1954: 931).[118] One may even agree with FISHER's rejection of BÖHM-BAWERK's distinction between an explanation of the positivity of the rate of interest and an explanation of its size and yet accept the question of the *existence* of the mere phenomenon of interest (positive or negative) as an additional independent aspect of the interest problem. In fact, this is what FISHER will be seen to have implicitly done.

The proposition made here is that the pure time preference theory should be reinterpreted as an explanation of nothing but these essentialist aspects of the in-

[118] SCHUMPETER did not emphasize the *independence* of this aspect of Böhm-Bawerk's theory, however.

terest phenomenon.[119] Such reinterpretation is indeed, as emphasized by KIRZNER and seen in Chapter 1 above, in the best tradition of Austrian subjectivist economics. On the view here proposed, it is an insight into the *essence* of the interest phenomenon pure time preference theorists have been emphasizing, not an insight into its quantitative aspects. A *pure* time preference theory does not (and, we believe, *cannot*) encompass an explanation of the general positivity of the rate of interest, let alone an explanation of the determination of the size of that rate. If it is indeed true, as KIRZNER was cited above (Section 8.4) as saying, that "all PTPT insists on is that, no matter how significant a role physical productivity may play among the complete list of variables affecting the rate of interest, it is fallacious to refer to interest income ... as the fruit of the physical productivity of agents of production" (KIRZNER 1993: 186), pure time preference theorists should have little problem with such reinterpretation.

The reinterpretation here suggested does, however, imply some further reconsideration of the pure time preference theory, particularly as concerns its history. First, perhaps, the adjective "pure" should be dropped, not only lest the theory should be associated with the view that a change in productivity conditions will have no effect whatsoever on the size of the rate of interest, but also lest it should be associated with the view that it is *not* perhaps eventually due also to the technical structure of the physical world around us that interest rates have in competitive economies generally tended to be positive. At least in its present form, the time preference theory proves nothing of the kind. Perhaps even the designation "time preference theory" is not an entirely happy one since it suggests that time preference alone, *rather than subjective time preference and objective productivity conditions together*, explains sign and size of the rate of interest. BÖHM-BAWERK's appellation "agio theory of interest" has the advantage of carrying no such misleading conotation. It has the further advantage of indicating unequivocally what has been called the "*locus classicus*" of the theory.

This *locus classicus* is indeed clearly to be found in BÖHM-BAWERK's *Positive Theory*, but in a more emphatic sense than has been explicitly acknowledged by either MISES or ROTHBARD; it is the focus on subjectivist criticism of (BÖHM-BAWERK-based) modern Austrian capital and interest theory (and thus on the *negative* elements of the time preference theory) that has kept more recent subjectivist contributions to the time preference theory from adequately acknowledging how eminent BÖHM-BAWERK's role for the development of the positive ele-

[119] This is not to say, of course, that the *negative* elements of the pure time preference theory, i.e., the criticism of other explanations of sign or size of the rate of interest, cannot be upheld or are not themselves important aspects of the theory.

ments of the time preference theory really is. His reformulation of the interest phenomenon as one of intertemporal exchange is the one central element common to all the versions of the time preference theory here considered. As to the more quantitive aspects of BÖHM-BAWERK's interest theory it must be noted that, however justified criticism of these aspects may have been, pure time preference theorists have significantly failed to provide what could be considered a sound alternative.

FETTER's analysis of these aspects, in particular, is all but nonexistent - in spite of his explicit assertion that it is in an explanation of these quantitative aspects of the interest problem that the positive theory of interest must be considered to consist. FETTER does not provide an explanation of the determination of the size of the rate of interest, and his explanation of the positivity of the sign of the rate of interest - as far as there can be said to be any such explanation at all - is no more than an unsystematic rehash of some elements of BÖHM-BAWERK's "psychological" grounds. His whole treatment is thus far below the standard set in BÖHM-BAWERK's *Positive Theory*. MISES also fails to address the question of the determination of the size of the rate of interest. But he does present us with a systematic treatment of the question of the general positivity of its sign which is in direct opposition, however, not only to BÖHM-BAWERK's, but also to FETTER's psychologism. In his attempt to deduce the positivity of the rate of time preference (and thus of the rate of interest) "praxeologically" from the axiom of human action, he unfortunately introduces a confusion into the concept of time preference - which he applies to subjective satisfactions rather than to objective goods, or money - which is instrumental in invalidating his analysis. The confusion is deepened by ROTHBARD - who implicitly interprets MISES "same" satisfactions as "one and the same" satisfaction - and perpetuated in more recent Austrian subjectivist contributions. It is this confusion that has led Austrian subjectivists to cling almost unanimously to the mistaken belief that they have indeed succeeded in explaining the general positivity of the rate of interest - *by time preference alone*. The most glaring hiatus finally is ROTHBARD's extension of this conclusion - also perpetuated in at least some more recent contributions, especially by O'DRISCOLL and GARRISON, and contradicted only by KIRZNER - to the question of the determination of the size of the rate of interest. It is this extension more than any other aspect of the pure time preference theory that has been responsible for "clogging the channels of communication" (YEAGER)[120] between Austrian subjectivist and mainstream economists.

120 Expression used in unpublished correspondence with GARRISON, ca. 1986)

Pure time preference theorists' attempts to explain the sign and the size of the rate of interest have not only been unsuccessfull. They have also involved them in many contradictions. These do not only concern - surprisingly - the very definition of time preference itself.[121] They also concern, for instance, - and this is closely related to the definition of the concept of time preference - the ice-in-winter/ice-in-summer example. Whereas for FETTER, this was an example of the fact that time preference is precisely not *always* in favor of present as opposed to future goods, MISES and ROTHBARD deny that this can be considered an example of time preference at all. But their arguments differ significantly: Whereas for MISES the two goods cannot be considered the same because they require different processes of production, ROTHBARD asserts that they cannot be so considered because they provide different satisfactions. (GARRISON seems implicitly to side with MISES on this, cf. Section 7.2.) A further point of contradiction is the question of the effect of a rise in physical productivity. Whereas FETTER predicts that this will lower the rate of interest, ROTHBARD asserts that a rise in physical productivity will not affect the rate of interest at all. KIRZNER does not exclude that it will *affect* the rate of interest, whereas GARRISON (adducing FISHER's reasons, not FETTER's) contends that it *might* actually lower that rate.

In our view, any reasonable prediction about the effect of a change in physical productivity on the rate of interest would require a much broader theoretical basis than Austrian subjectivists have in effect been supplying. Their failure to do so is probably a result of their belief that they have succeeded in explaining the phenomenon of interest exhaustively by time preference alone. If our analysis is not mistaken, this belief has turned out to be untenable. Either Austrian subjectivists must reform their analysis to include an investigation of the relationship between productivity conditions and the explanation of the positivity of the sign and the determination of the size of the rate of interest - a reform which does perhaps not necessarily compel them to revoke their view that interest is the market reflection of individual time preference conditions - or they must declare that, being merely a theory of the *essence* of interest, the time preference theory is not concerned with these more empirical questions. Whichever option they choose, Austrian subjectivists must take into consideration that the time preference theory is part of the Austrian subjectivist theory of value in general: the interpretation put upon a subjectivist theory of interest has direct implications for the interpretation put upon a subjectivist theory of price. In fact, this parallelism has sometimes

121 In view of the fact that, as we have seen, none of the pure time preference theorists really provides us with a *definition* of the concept of time preference, it may perhaps be said to be not quite correct to speak of "contradictions." Contradictions may be said to be impied, however, in the different meanings implied in the use made of the concept.

(although surprisingly rarely) been explicitly observed. Thus O'DRISCOLL has (somewhat mistakenly) deplored that, following FISHER,

> "... modern treatments of interest rate determination eschew the question of why equilibrium interest rates must be positive, focusing instead on the determinants of market rates. The question of the 'nature and necessity' of a positive rate is treated as an arcane issue. ... Yet in price theory the necessity of dealing with the 'nature and necessity' of positive prices for consumables is recognized." (1979: 20)

To the extent that we can indeed observe a tendency away from an interest in the investigation of the nature or essence of economic phenomena towards an interest in the investigation of the main determinants of the size of these phenomena - a tendency that does perhaps go hand in hand with a tendency away from a focus on the "understanding" of these phenomena towards a focus on their "control" -, however, this tendency can be observed in *both* fields.[122] Moreover, O'DRISCOLL obviously presumes that "the question of why equilibrium interest rates must be positive" is satisfactorily answered in the time preference theory. This, as we have seen, is not the case. Nor can we see how "the 'nature and necessity' of positive prices" can possibly be demonstrated by subjective considerations, i.e., marginal utility, *alone*.

It remains for us to indicate that, however Austrian subjectivists may choose to reformulate the time preference theory of interest, such reformulation does not necessarily impair the relevance they have often claimed for their theory in the context of at least one recent debate in economic theory, viz., the Cambridge controversy in the theory of capital and interest (KIRZNER 1983, 1993: 188-91; cf. O'DRISCOLL 1979: 1-2, 40-1).[123] The neglect of the time preference theory in this debate has been claimed to have had "the unfortunate effect of gravely misrepresenting the relevant available theoretical alternatives" (KIRZNER 1983: 2) - the time preference theory presenting a third, presumably superior, alternative. This alternative shares important insights with both the Cambridge U.S. and the Cam-

---

122 Indeed, I cannot see that in modern price theory "the necessity of dealing with 'the nature and necessity' of positive prices for consumables is recognized" prior to a theory of the determination of the size of the prices for these consumables.

123 Austrian subjectivists have claimed relevance for their theory of interest in at least two other contexts: One is the revival of BÖHM-BAWERK-based Austrian capital theory since the seventies (O'Driscoll 1979: 1-2) mentioned in Chapter 1. The other (KIRZNER 1983a) is a type of criticism that has driven one recent (non-subjectivist) commentator (having carefully reviewed the major alternative theoretical approaches to the explanation of interest) to the dramatic conclusion that "economists do not understand the phenomena of capital and interest. They do not understand why the rate of interest is generally positive (and thus how it is that capitalism can work). ... Of course, they are not totally ignorant about any of these problems. ... Yet our ignorance remains vast." (HAUSMAN 1981: 191, cited in KIRZNER 1983a) The time preference theory, presumably, is regarded as invulnerable to this criticism.

bridge U.K. views on the phenomenon of interest. For in the Austrian subjectivist view, the phenomenon of interest, although decidedly a market exchange phenomenon,[124] is emphatically not to be seen as the payment for the services of a factor of production.[125] It is thus not vulnerable to the capital-reversal paradoxes:

> "These paradoxes seem to offer challenges to the neo-classical view ... solely because that view sees interest as a productivity return; for a theory which ... attributes no role at all to 'productivity,' no such challenge is to be discovered." (KIRZNER 1983: 30)

Thus, even in the reformulation here offered, the Austrian subjectivist theory of interest may yet turn out not be entirely irrelevant to modern economic theory.

---

124 This view, associated with Cambridge (U.S.), has been emphatically denied by the Cambridge (U.K.) theorists: "Modern Ricardian theory puts a good deal of emphasis on the fact that the payments to capital are dispositions of a surplus and do not involve any kind of exchange. There simply is no corresponding stream moving in the opposite direction." (NELL 1967: 200; cited in Kirzner 1983: 8)

125 Kirzner sees this as the essence of the Cambridge (U.S.) position: "The neo-classical view sees interest received by the owners of capital as revenue obtained through the sale, to producers, of the services of a special kind. Interest emerges as the price *necessary* to be paid in order to persuade the owners of capital to make these resource services available; it is able to be offered by producers because the use of these productive services permits an output larger than would have otherwise been possible." (1983: 5) It is this view that is effectively called into question by the reswitching paradox: "The initial result of no general relationship between rate of profit and value of capital goods per man came to contradict the marginal-theory interpretation of the rate of profit as a selector of capital-intensity, i.e., as an 'index of scarcity' of the 'quantity of capital'" (PASINETTI 1969: 283, cited in KIRZNER 1983: 31).

Chapter 9

Appendix:
Irving FISHER's "Impatience Theory of Interest"

In the foregoing, we have suggested that the Austrian subjectivist "pure time preference theory of interest" should be interpreted not as an explanation of the positivity of the sign, nor as a theory of the determination of the size of the rate of interest, but as a theory of the mere existence of such a rate (be it positive or negative), or, to use the old-fashioned phrase, as a theory of the "essence" of the phenomenon of interest and its corollary, laborless income. As such, it overlaps with what we have claimed to be a part of, rather than presenting an alternative to, BÖHM-BAWERK's agio theory - properly interpreted as encompassing not only a theory of the sign and size of the rate of interest, but an underlying reinterpretation of the phenomenon of interest as one of time preference. A theory of interest may be a time preference, or agio theory, we have argued, in spite of whatever emphasis it may accord to technical productivity conditions in explaining the general positivity of the sign or the determination of the size of the rate of interest in a market economy.

With such a reinterpretation, many more theories of interest may perhaps properly be regarded as time preference or agio theories. MISES himself was seen to have named JEVONS, WICKSELL, and FISHER as time preference theorists (1949: 485-6, cited in Chapter 5), whereas FISHER in his turn mentions RAE (1834; cf. MIXTER 1905), JEVONS (1870), LAUNHARDT (1885) and SAX (1887) as precursers, and Knut WICKSELL (1893) and Adolphe LANDRY (1904) as direct followers, among others, of BÖHM-BAWERK's agio theory (cf. FISHER 1907: 54, 74, 1911: 385).[126] SCHUMPETER again was seen (Chapter 2n) to have emphasized FISHER's contribution in working out the implications of what we have interpreted as the essentialist aspect and what he significantly emphasized as "perhaps the most important of all" aspects of the agio theory. It is surely no coincidence that it is in reaction to FISHER's statement of the agio theory, and not to FETTER's earlier and considerably more pronounced statement, that the first debate of the pure time preference theory developed (SEAGER 1912, FISHER 1913, SEAGER 1913, BROWN 1913, FETTER 1914, BROWN 1914, FETTER 1914a).[127] FISHER's impa-

[126] FISHER also makes general mention of some medieval writers putting emphasis on *mora* (delay), and of the abstinence theory of Nassau SENIOR and others (1907: 54). Strangely, however, he makes no mention of FETTER.

[127] According to FETTER himself, the paper by Seager (1912), written in reaction to FISHER's presentation of "The 'Impatience Theory' of Interest" in his *Principles of Economics* (1912; cf. 1911), is "the first systematic attempt that has been made to disprove any ver-

tience theory of interest is indeed of exemplary significance in the context of the present enquiry, for reasons to be investigated in some detail in the present chapter.

FISHER regards his theory, as first developed in *The Rate of Interest* (1907), subsequently summarized in "The 'Impatience Theory' of Interest" (1911) as well as in his *Principles of Economics* (1912), and finally reformulated without substantial (merely expository) change in *The Theory of Interest* (1930), as a "form of" (1907: 87, cited below) or "modification of Böhm-Bawerk's agio theory" (1911: 386). He characterizes the latter as follows:

> "Böhm-Bawerk's theory is called by him the 'agio theory' of interest, *since it finds the essence of the rate of interest in the agio or premium on present goods when exchanged for future goods*. This theory is in the main accepted by the present writer as the natural and proper starting-point for any rational discussion of the subject." (1907: 53, e.a.)

One modification concerns BÖHM-BAWERK's third cause, the technical superiority of present over future goods, which FISHER "believe(s) to contain essential errors" (1907: 55). The first two causes are "undoubtedly pertinent and will be incorporated, under a somewhat different form, in the theory of the present book" (1907: 55). We immediately note, however, that FISHER promises, for his own theory,

> "... the formulation of the exact manner in which the 'technique' or actual conditions of production enter into the determination of interest." (1907: 74)

A modification considered by FISHER to be even more fundamental regards his redefinition of the concept of time preference in terms of subjective "enjoyment income:"

> "Our presentation may, in fact, be classified as a form of the agio theory, differing from Böhm-Bawerk's version chiefly in the omission of 'the technical advantage of present over future goods,' and from agio theories in general by the explicit introduction of the income-concept. *The income-concept plays the central role*." (1907: 87-8, e.a.; cf. vii, 1930: ix, 13)[128]

---

sion of the newer (psychological, as opposed to technological, I.P.) theory of interest" (1914: 226). FETTER exempts "adverse criticism in scattered book reviews and in occasional footnotes" (ibid.), without providing references, however.

128 SEAGER has emphasized the importance of another modification which concerns FISHER's concept of capital: "Professor Fisher's 'Impatience Theory of Interest' is Professor Eugen von Böhm-Bawerk's 'Discount Theory,' with two highly important modifications. Fisher denies the validity of the distinction between land and capital (that is, 'produced means of further production') and refuses to admit that what Böhm-Bawerk calls the 'technical superiority of present over future goods' and what other writers have characterized more briefly as 'productivity of capital' has any influence on the comparison between present gratifications and future gratifications in which, as he believes, the complete and final explanation of interest is to be sought." (SEAGER 1912: 834) FISHER indeed regards any source of enjoyment income as capital (i.e., capitalized income). The notion of capital thus includes not only land, but also human beings and even goods of immediate consumption. *Every* source of income, for FISHER, is capital, and any income is to be regarded as interest on capital, including wages and land rent: "Hence interest is not a part, but the whole, of

We briefly review FISHER's criticism of BÖHM-BAWERK's reasoning in support of his third ground. Note, however, that we are not here concerned with this criticism in and of itself; for this would take us into the details of the negative elements of the time preference theory, i.e., its criticism of other theories of interest, with which, as we said at the outset, we would not be primarily concerned. Yet, as will be seen, FISHER's criticism does contain one element at least which may, after all, not be entirely irrelevant to the construction of a "positive" time preference theory. This element should thus not go unnoticed in a chapter dealing with the extent to which FISHER may be regarded as a time preference theorist.

In BÖHM-BAWERK's reasoning in support of his third cause, FISHER distinguishes "three principal steps:"

> "In the reasoning by which Böhm-Bawerk attempts to prove his 'technical superiority,' there are three principal steps. The first consists of postulating an 'average production period' representing the length of the productive processes of a community; the second consists of the proposition that the longer this average production period, the greater will be the product; and the third consists in the conclusion that in consequence of this greater productiveness of lengthy processes, present goods possess a 'technical superiority' over future goods. We shall endeavor to show that the third of these steps contains a fatal error. The first step also is not wholly satisfactory." (1907: 55)

Having noted some difficulties with the first step,[129] FISHER names FETTER (1902a: 13 passim) foremost among those who "have criticized Böhm-Bawerk's concept of a production period so fully that we need not mention additional perplexities" (1907: 58). FISHER's acute and (to the present writer's opinion) conclusive criticism of the "third and crucial step" (1907: 58, cf. 58-74) has been the object of a lengthy and largely confused reply by BÖHM-BAWERK (III: Essay XII, esp. 162-83; cf. above, Chapter 2n).[130] Again citing FETTER's indictment of

---

income. It includes what is called rents and profits, and even wages; for the income of the workman may be capitalized as truely as the income of land or machinery. Thus, so far from having 'interest, rent, wages, and profits' as mutually exclusive portions of income, we see that 'interest' includes all four." (1907: 229-30)

129 FISHER mentions the arbitrariness of the method of averaging, the difficulty of collapsing average periods for different industries into an average period for the economy as a whole, the extension of the absolute period of production into the indefinite past, and the fact that the construction of an index would itself involve a rate of interest (1907: 56-8). In an appended "Case Illustrating Futility of Measuring Average Production Period" (1907: 352-3), he also develops a simple example of a reswitching of techniques (cf. VELAPILLAI 1975), viz., a case of two techniques of which one "would, oddly enough, be the most economical if the rate of interest were either very high or very low, whereas the other alternative would be chosen in case the interest were at a more moderate rate" so that "it is not true that one of the alternatives will be chosen if the rate of interest is high, and the other if the rate of interest is low, as would be the case if they were subject to Böhm-Bawerk's series" (1907: 352).

130 This essay "On the Relationship Between the 'Third Reason' for Higher Valuation of Present Goods and the Two Other Reasons" (III: 150-93) is by far the longest in his *Further*

BÖHM-BAWERK's third cause (1902a: 185, cited Chapter 4 above), FISHER concludes in precisely the same vein:

> "His theory of technical superiority stands out as incongruous with the rest of his work, and is more in keeping with the productivity theories which he has done so much to demolish. It would seem as though, like a successful warrior, he has been haunted by the ghost of his slain enemies." (1907: 73)

The second step, "to which no objection is offered" (1907: 58) in the main text of *The Rate of Interest*, is the object of a clarificatory appendix, however, "Showing how Periods of Production which are Relatively Long but Unproductive are Eliminated" (1907: 353-4). Here FISHER presents the following argument:

> "That long processes (assuming their length to be measurable) are more productive than short processes is, as Böhm-Bawerk says, a general fact, not a necessary truth. The reason lies in *selection*. It is not true that of all *possible* production processes the longest are the most productive; but it is true that, of all productive processes *actually employed*, the longest are also the most productive. ... Suppose that by means of 100 days' labor invested to-day we can obtain a product of 100 units one year hence, or of 250 two years hence, of 50 three years hence, of 300 four years hence, of 250 five years hence, of 320 six years hence, of 100 seven years hence, of 300 eight years hence, etc., - a series which we take quite at random. Out of this series of choices there will be eliminated those of 3, 5, 7, and 8 years, for each of these is outclassed by preceding choices. ... Eliminating, then, these ineligible cases, we have left, to choose from, the 1, 2, 4, and 6 year periods." (1907: 353)

Now, the reader will immediately recognize the significance of FISHER's argument in the context of the present investigation. Strangely, FISHER himself never elaborated this significance. But BÖHM-BAWERK rightly interpreted FISHER's clarification as proof that FISHER, "inspite of his formal approval, materially denies my thesis" (III: 45); for FISHER's appendix creates the impression that

> "... an objective rule based on natural and technical reasons[131] does not exist at all, but that we are deceived into an assumption of such a rule by our own selection" (III: 49)

- a selection, we must significantly add, that is based on a systematic preference for present over future goods. The whole argument has obvious implications for the debate between a pure time preference and a time preference cum productivity explanation of interest, implications that were not spelt out by either FISHER *or* BÖHM-BAWERK. But the wording and sheer length of BÖHM-BAWERK's Essay IV "Concerning the Bearing of 'Selection' on the Greater Productivity of Longer

---

Essays, i.e., in the third volume of the fourth edition of *Capital and Interest*. It is a prime example of BÖHM-BAWERK's well-known mastery of what he himself called (with reference to others) "abstract dialectics" and "scholastic reasoning" (III: 151, 175). To the present writer's knowledge, a detailed analysis of the debate between BÖHM-BAWERK and FISHER (including the latter's reaction to BÖHM-BAWERK's essay (1930: 473-85)) has never been undertaken. It would show that BÖHM-BAWERK's arguments are largely incorrect, inconclusive, and mutually contradictory.

131 Note that in developing his proposed rule BÖHM-BAWERK made much of such "natural and technical reasons" (cf. II: 3-15; cf. 1900 and III: Essay I).

Roundabout Methods of Production" (III: 45-56)[132] suggests that he was not entirely unaware of them: If "objective" productivity conditions turn out to be "subjective" time preference conditions "in disguise," then this would perforce be an argument in favor of a "purely" subjective theory of interest. Surprisingly, the argument is not taken up anywhere, to the present writer's knowledge, in the literature on the time preference theory that has been under investigation.[133] It shall thus not concern us beyond our noting its presence in FISHER's *Rate of Interest*.

We have already become acquainted with FISHER's other modification, viz., his redefinition of the concept of time preference in terms of subjective "psychic" or "enjoyment income," approximated in terms of money (cf. Chapter 3 above). With the rate of the preference for present over future enjoyable income considered "the subjective prototype of the rate of interest" (1907: 234) and the rate of preference between any two periods depending (principally) on the character of the *entire* future income stream (1907: 92), the explanation of the (determination of the size of the) rate of interest (we recall that FISHER was seen to have rejected BÖHM-BAWERK's distinction between an explanation of the determination of the size and an explanation of the positivity of the sign of the rate of interest)[134] becomes co-extensive with an explanation of the choice of the intertemporal income stream:

---

[132] To the present writer's knowledge, the dispute between FISHER and BÖHM-BAWERK has never been investigated in detail. It is perhaps noteworthy that in his later *Theory of Interest*, FISHER not only omits his clarification of BÖHM-BAWERK's rule, but also obscures it by emphasizing some minor agreement on the point in question: "Böhm-Bawerk himself," FISHER here writes, "in his reply to my original criticism, asserts his agreement with my contention concerning the second step that, while long processes are in general more productive than short processes, this is not a universal truth. Of the infinite number of possible longer processes only those that are more productive than shorter ones are chosen." (1930: 475-6) However, the main issue was not, as FISHER's comment would suggest, whether the greater productivity of more roundabout methods is a universal truth or not, i.e., whether processes that are longer are *always* more productive (which both BÖHM-BAWERK and FISHER agree they are *not*), but, as BÖHM-BAWERK had pointed out, whether the fact that there is generally a longer process which is more productive is a *technological* rule, or "whether we are deceived into an assumption of such a rule by our own selection."

[133] An argument similar to FISHER's has been advanced by Professor KIRZNER (without reference to FISHER), however, in private discussion with the present writer. To the latter's best memory, KIRZNER posited the case of an island covered by forest (some trees carrying fruit) on which an outcast is dropped at random. Seen "objectively" from above, the forest shows no technological regularity whatsoever. Yet the outcast will "subjectively" perceive the following rule: he can either pick a given amount of fruit from the fruit tree nearest to his reach; or he can, at the expense of time, make his way to fruit trees carrying more, or better fruit, lying farther away. To him, the farther he will travel, the more opulent the fruit supply he will be able to appropriate.

[134] We shall shortly see that FISHER does not really succeed in conflating these two issues.

> "The solution here offered is that the rate of interest depends on the character of the income-stream ... and above all its distribution in time. It might be called a theory of *prospective provision of income*." (1907: viii)

But the rate of time preference depends not only on the character of the income stream - in addition to time shape FISHER lists size,[135] composition,[136] and probability as its most highly important characteristics (1907: 92-102) - but also on the character of the individual - here FISHER lists foresight, self control, habit, expectation of life, and interest in the lives of other persons as important characteristics (1907: 102-9). FISHER's declared emphasis on time-shape suggests that the first set of characterictics be identified roughly with BÖHM-BAWERK's first reason (FISHER 1907: 98, BÖHM-BAWERK III: 183-4), while the second set of circumstances is akin to those emphasized in the context of BÖHM-BAWERK's second reason. FISHER subsumes the second reason under the first, however, by way of what BÖHM-BAWERK has called "the rather mysterious formula" (III: 185) that "these other factors (the second set of circumstances, I.P.) may conveniently be regarded as affecting the 'form of function' which expresses its (time preference's, I.P.) dependence on income" (1907: 103; cf. 109).[137],[138]

FISHER develops his theory of the determination of *The Rate of Interest* in three approximations: In the first he assumes "that each individual is initially possessed of a foreknown (*money*, I.P.) income-stream" which is both "certain and fixed" (1907: 118). Fixity implies that "the capital-instruments which he possesses are each capable of only a single definite series of services contributing to his income-stream" (1907: 118), whereas certainty implies that no risk attaches to the different income elements. However, the individual "is free to exchange any part of it" by borrowing or lending (1907: 118; cf. 1930: 99-101). The resultant *enjoyment* income stream is chosen so as to maximize present desirability. FISHER successively relaxes the assumptions of fixity and certainty of the income stream in the second and third approximations. Only the first two approximations

---

135 The larger the general level of income, argues FISHER, the less urgent the preference for present income (1907: 95). This is the reason why FISHER predicts that a general rise in physical productivity will, via an increase in the general level of income, lower the rate of interest (1913: 613-5; cf. Chapter 4 above).

136 Expression of time preference in terms of homogeneous enjoyable income saves FISHER from the necessity of taking the composition of the income stream into explicit consideration (1907: 99).

137 Quite misleadingly, FISHER a few pages earlier equates his concept of time preference "very nearly (with, I.P.) what Böhm-Bawerk calls the 'perspective undervaluation of the future'" (1907: 88), i.e., with BÖHM-BAWERK's second reason (cf. BÖHM-BAWERK III: 184n76). Possibly, this statement foreshadows FISHER's later unhappy replacement of the notion of time preference by the notion of impatience, which is indeed remindful of BÖHM-BAWERK's "perspective undervaluation of the future."

138 Cf. note above. FISHER's formula is not quite so mysterious, perhaps, if the notion of "function" is understood (as it was undoubtedly meant) in the mathematical sense.

are relevant to the present investigation. FISHER presents each approximation first in words, and then in geometric and algebraic terms. In the following, we shall concentrate on his geometric presentation, the well-known FISHER-diagram.[139]

Figure 1 can be used to demonstrate both individual and market adjustment, under the assumptions of FISHER's first approximation, for the case of two individuals, A and B, and two periods, say, "this year" and "next year."[140]:

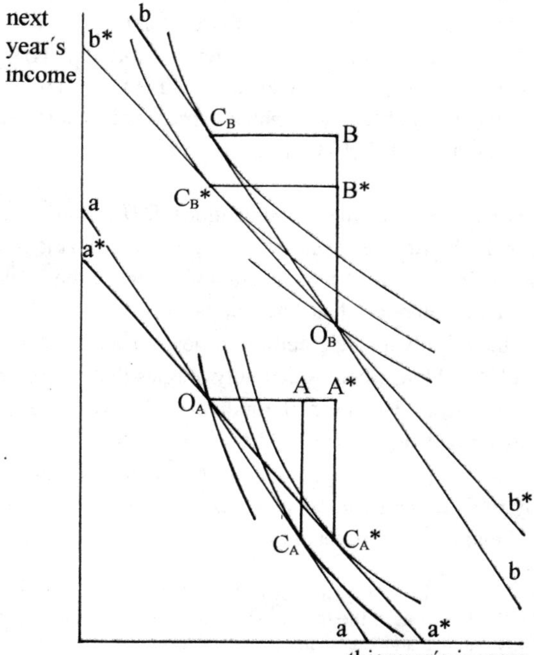

Figure 1: FISHER's First Approximation to the Determination of the Rate of Interest (cf. 1907: 387, 394, and passim, 1930: 254 and passim; cf. also CONARD 1959: 50-2 and Fig.I)

---

[139] Apart from the extension of the analysis to n periods, FISHER's algebraic presentation, which is based on a count of equations and unknowns, adds nothing of significance for the purposes of the present investigation.

[140] Income for all other periods is regarded as fixed and unalterable (1907: 374, 1930: 235).

This year's income is laid off along the horizontal axis and next year's income along the vertical axis.[141] Both are measured in money units. O_A and O_B represent A's and B's original *money* income position with respect to the two periods under consideration. One of a family of intertemporal indifference curves (drawn with respect to hypothetical *enjoyment* income combinations)[142] for individual A passes through O_A, and one for individual B passes through O_B. Both are drawn convex to the origin, representing a decreasing rate of time preference, or impatience, with increasing provision with this year's relative to next year's income.[143]

For a given market rate of interest, all possible *enjoyment* income combinations attainable by individual A through borrowing or lending are represented by a straight interest line aa drawn through O_A, and all possible enjoyment income combinations for individual B by a parallel interest line bb drawn through O_B. Both interest lines are drawn with an absolute slope greater than one, representing the possibility of exchanging a given amount of present income for a larger amount of future income, and thus a positive market rate of interest. In their original positions, A is assumed to display a rate of time preference or impatience greater, and B one lower, than the market rate of interest. Individual adjustment can now be demonstrated by a movement from O_A to C_A, representing maximum present desirability (the highest attainable indifference curve), for individual A, and by a movement from O_B to C_B, representing maximum present desirability, for individual B. A, who had a rate of impatience higher than the market rate of interest, wishes to borrow AO_A of present income in exchange for AC_A of future income, whereas B, who had a rate of impatience lower than the market rate of interest, wishes to lend BC_B of present income in exchange for BO_B of future income. Such adjustment of the time shape of the income stream will lower the rate of impatience for individual A, and raise the rate of impatience for individual B. Figure 1 demonstrates geometrically the fact that individual adjustment to a given

---

141 FISHER assumes moreover "that the income of each year is concentrated at some point, say the middle of the year, making the two such points just a year apart, and that borrowing and lending are so restricted as to affect only this year's and next year's income" (1907: 374; cf. 1930: 288).

142 FISHER speaks of "iso-desirability" (1907: 389 and passim), and later of "willingness" (1930: 238 and passim; cf. 245n6), or "impatience" (e.g. 1930: 260) lines.

143 In view of his later relacement of the notion of time preference by that of "impatience" (1911) - with impatience regarded as "a fundamental attribute of human nature" (1911: 387, cf. Chapter 4 above and this chapter below) - we take note of the fact that FISHER here explicitly admits negative rates of time preference: "The fact that the iso-desirability curves at the right slope less than 45^0," he writes, "interprets the fact, which should not be lost sight of, that if this year's income is sufficiently abundant and next year's income sufficiently scarce, or both, that this year's goods may exchange for next year's on less than even terms; that is, that the rate of time-preference may be negative." (1907: 390)

market rate of interest leads to equality of the marginal rates of time preference or impatience to each other and to the rate of interest.[144]

Figure 1 can also be used to demonstrate market equilibrium. In the situation characterized by interest lines aa and bb and equilibrium points C_A for individual A and C_B for individual B, the demand for this year's income, AO_A, is smaller than the supply of this year's income, BC_B, and the demand for next year's income, BO_B, is larger than the supply, AC_A. Under such conditions of excess supply of this year's income and excess demand for next year's income, the rate of interest will tend to fall. Interest lines a^*a^* and b^*b^* are drawn more nearly horizontal to represent a possible equilibrium market rate of interest. With the lower rate of interest, the new points of maximum desirability, $C_A{}^*$ and $C_B{}^*$, are such that A's demand for this year's income, $A^*O_A{}^*$, equals B's supply of this year's income, $B^*C_B{}^*$, and B's demand for next year's income, $B^*O_B{}^*$, equals A's supply of next year's income, $A^*C_A{}^*$. As can be seen, since market equilibration implies individual equilibration, the individual marginal rates of impatience are again equal to each other and to the rate of interest. As FISHER emphasizes, the geometric demonstration can be extended to three periods, using willingness surfaces and interest planes (1907: 394, 1930: 254). It can also be extended, in principle at least, to any number of individuals.[145] FISHER interprets his analysis as demonstrating that (at least under the assumptions of the first approximation) individual rates of time preference are the "cause" of the rate of interest:

> "Thus far we have regarded the individual only, and have seen that he conforms his rate of preference to the rate of interest. For him, the rate of interest is a relatively fixed fact, since his own time-preference and resulting action can influence it only infinitesimally. His rate of preference is the variable. In

---

144 FISHER notes the parallelism between the individual adjustment process in intertemporal exchange and the individual adjustment process in atemporal exchange in which buying or selling at a given market price affects the provision with goods until (relative) marginal rates of utility conform to (relative) price (1907: 119, 1911: 392, 1930: 119-20).

145 FISHER's algebraic presentation of his first approximation to the determination of the rate of interest (1907: 374-94, 1930: 288-301) has the advantage that the analysis can be extended to any number of periods. FISHER acknowledges that if there are n periods there is not one but n-1 rates of interest - one between each pair of successive time periods. Criticizing BÖHM-BAWERK's assertion of a tendency to make these rates equal, he argues: "If the total enjoyable income of society would be foreknown to be, in the ensuing year, 10 billion dollars, in the following year one billion, and in the third year 20 billion, and there were no way of avoiding these enormous disparities, it is very evident that the income of the middle year would have a very high valuation compared with either of its neighbors, and therefore that the rate of interest connecting that middle year with the first year would be very low, whereas that connecting it with the third year would be very high." (1907: 384; cf. 1930: 299-301) Note that, in spite of his occasional remarks that the rate of time preference may for an appropriate time shape of the income stream also be negative (cf. note above), even in the extreme case here posited FISHER does not explicitly acknowledge the possibility of a negative rate of interest.

> short, for him individually the rate of interest is cause, and the rate of preference, effect. For society as a whole, however, the order of cause and effect is reversed." (1907: 130; cf. 1911: 396, 1930: 119-21)

Once more drawing the parallel to the general theory of price, FISHER continues:

> "This change is like the corresponding inversion of cause and effect in the theory of prices. Each individual regards the market price, say, of sugar, as fixed, and adjusts his marginal utility to it; whereas, for the entire group forming the market, we know that the price of sugar is due to its marginal utility to the consumer (cf. FISHER 1892: 28). In the same way, while for the individual the rate of interest determines the rate of preference, for society the rates of preference of the individuals determine the rate of interest. The rate of interest is simply the rate of preference, upon which the whole community may concur in order that the market of loans may be exactly cleared. ... Thus, *the rate of interest is the common market rate of preference for present over future income*, as determined by the supply and demand of present and future income. ... (T)he foregoing discussion gives us a complete theory of the causes which determine the rate of interest, or rather, the *rates* of interest for various time periods." (1907: 130-2, e.a.; cf. 1911: 396, 1930: 119-21)[146]

In his second approximation, FISHER relaxes the assumption of fixity of the income stream; there are now assumed to be different options with regard to the use to which capital instruments can be put, each option yielding a different intertemporal money income stream (1907: 137). In keeping with his criticism of BÖHM-BAWERK's proposed rule of the greater productivity of more roundabout methods of production, FISHER first seems to assume a distribution of options quite at random. Some of these options, however, will consist of income elements none of which is greater, and at least one of which is smaller, than the corresponding element of some other income stream. These will not be chosen under any circumstances and are therefore termed - not quite correctly - "ineligible" (1907: 150). Concerning the remaining "eligible" options, FISHER then enunciates a "law of decreasing returns for additional sacrifice:"

> "Thus, the farmer may cultivate his farm with any degree of intensity; and for each particular degree of intensity, he will have a different income-stream. He may, for instance, invest \$100 worth of labor in the present, in order that in six months he may have a larger income than otherwise, by S200. If the rate of interest is 4 per cent (reckoned semi-annually), he would evidently prefer this option; for it diminishes his present income by \$100 and increase his income six months later by \$200, being 100 per cent in six months, whereas the interest for that time is only 2 per cent. Another course would be to invest, not \$100, but \$200, in present cultivation. The extra \$100 would add to his returns in a half-year's time something less than the \$200 yielded on his first \$100, let us say \$150. This also would be a good investment, yielding him 50 per cent return when the rate of interest is 2 per cent. And so each successive

---

146 FISHER nowhere acknowledges the problem involved in interpreting - in a system in which several endogenous variables are simultaneously determined - one endogenous variable as "causing" the other. In a system focused on the determination of the size of economic variables, only the exogenous variables, it seems, can be interpreted as "causes" of the endogenous variables of the system. In the case in question these would be the individuals' intertemporal preference structure on the one hand, and their original money income endowments on the other.

> choice, compared with its predecessor, shows a *law of decreasing returns for additional sacrifice*." (1907: 156-7)

Investment is advantageous as long as the rate of return on sacrifice - the excess of return over investment, as a percentage of the amount invested (cf. 1907: 152-6) - exceeds the rate of interest; for it then increases the present value of the income stream. This leads FISHER to

> "... the conclusion that ... the option chosen, compared with a neighboring option with which it was in competition, yields a rate of return on sacrifice equal to the rate of interest. This rate of return ... we shall call the *marginal rate of return on sacrifice*. It follows that, when there is a continuous range of choice, we may substitute for the statement that the choice will fall upon the option of maximum present worth, the better statement that the choice will fall on the option whose *marginal rate of return on sacrifice, reckoned relatively to a neighboring option, is equal to the rate of interest*." (1907: 158)

Figure 2 can be used to demonstrate both individual and market adjustment under the assumptions of FISHER's second approximation:

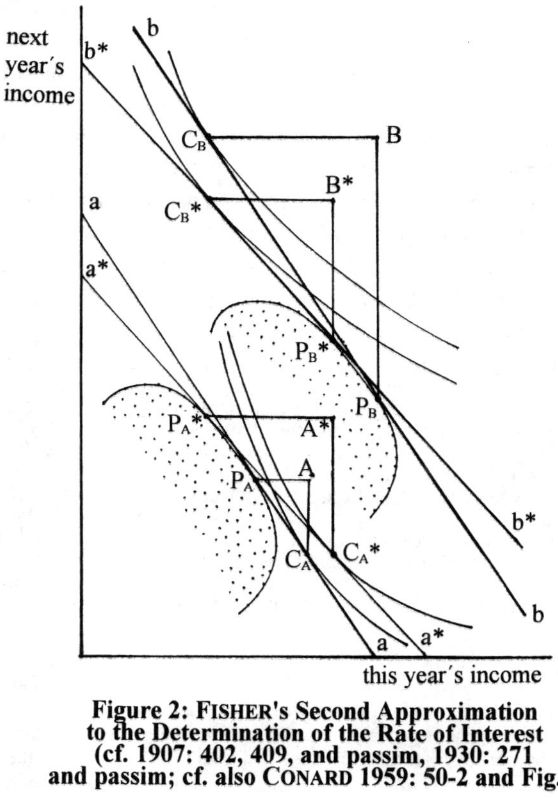

Figure 2: FISHER's Second Approximation to the Determination of the Rate of Interest (cf. 1907: 402, 409, and passim, 1930: 271 and passim; cf. also CONARD 1959: 50-2 and Fig.I)

Individuals A and B are now faced each with a swarm of alternative income combinations lying on or below the concave boundary $P_A P_A{}^*$, for individual A, and $P_B P_B{}^*$, for individual B. All eligible options lie on the negatively sloped parts of these "opportunity" boundaries. The concavity of the boundary is due to FISHER's "law of decreasing returns for additional sacrifice." For slopes of the boundary smaller than minus one the marginal rate of return is negative.

Each individual is now faced with a market rate of interest implicit in the slope of a swarm of parallel interest lines. Maximization of present desirability of the final enjoyment income stream implies that each will choose, out of the eligible money income combinations, the combination with the maximum present value, i.e., that combination which lies on the interest line farthest from the origin. This is indicated by the point of tangency of an interest line with the individual's opportunity line, P_A for individual A, and P_B for individual B.[147] The tangency condition is that the marginal rate of return on sacrifice for each individual is equal to the rate of interest. In keeping with the rate of interest, individual A will then demand AP_A units of present income in exchange for AC_A units of future income, and individual B will supply BC_B units of present income in exchange for BP_B units of future income.

At the rate of interest implicit in parallel interest lines aa and bb, A's demand for present income, AP_A, is smaller than B's supply of present income, BC_B, and B's demand for future income, BP_B, is greater than A's supply of future income, AC_A. The excess supply of present income and excess demand for future income would then tend to lower the rate of interest. A market equilibrium situation is characterized by parallel interest lines a*a* for individual A and b*b* for individual B, drawn more nearly horizontal to represent a lower rate of interest. Both individuals now adjust their money income positions as well as their enjoyment income positions. At the lower rate of interest both select money income positions providing for less present and more future income than at the higher rate of interest. Individual A then wishes to modify his money income position represented by $P_A{}^*$ by demanding $A^*P_A{}^*$ of present income in exchange for $A^*C_A{}^*$ of future income, and individual B wishes to modify his money income position represented by $P_B{}^*$ by offering $B^*C_B{}^*$ of present income in exchange for $B^*P_B{}^*$ of

147 Any other money income combination would necessarily lie on an interest line nearer to the origin. Any final enjoyment income position chosen would then be less desirable than some possible enjoyment income position on the interest line tangent to the boundary. Thus, "the condition of maximum desirability includes that of maximum present value" (1907: xxii; cf. 411-2).

future income. The intertemporal market now exactly clears. FISHER concludes his second approximation as follows:

> "We have introduced a new magnitude into our discussion; namely, the rate of return on sacrifice, and especially the particular value of this rate of return called the *marginal* rate of return on sacrifice. *This marginal rate of return on sacrifice comes close to being a 'natural rate of interest.'* By means of it we are enabled to admit into our theory the elements of truth contained in some of the claims of the productivity theories, the cost theories, and Böhm-Bawerk's theory of the technique of production." (1907: 159, e.a.)

Like BÖHM-BAWERK (cf. Chapter 2 above), FISHER likens his marginal rate of return on sacrifice to what others have called "the productivity of capital:"

> "The same illustrations which have been given will serve to set the present theory in line with that of Adolphe Landry in his *Théorie de l'Intérêt*. He states that one of the conditions determining the rate of interest is the 'productivity of capital,' in the peculiar sense which he gives to this phrase. The process described by Landry by which the productivity is assimilated to whatever rate of interest happens to rule the market, virtually corresponds to the successive selection of income-streams as outlined in the preceding examples." (1907: 161)

This, basically, is FISHER's theory (of the determination of) the rate of interest. It is not accepted by pure time preference theorists (cf. e.g. O'DRISCOLL 1979: 32-3) due to a problem explicitly noted by FISHER himself (1907: 167-75, 1930: 278-9). This is the fact that, if conceived in terms of money units, the opportunity line is not independent of the rate of interest itself:

> "Of course the *O* line cannot be drawn without the aid of valuations which involve ... the rate of interest. The farmer who encounters the law of diminishing returns in agriculture buys machinery and labor and sells grain. His *O* line is thus somewhat dependent on the prices of machinery and, since the price of every good is a discounted valuation, it depends on the rate of interest. ... Thus, strictly speaking, his *O* line is not to be pictured as immovable like a rock but as subject to some slight change with every change in the slope of the M (interest, I.P.) line." (1930: 278)

To FISHER this presents no problem, however, for his explanation of interest. For, since each rate of interest implies a definite opportunity line, the task remains of finding that rate of interest which clears the intertemporal market (1907: 174). The fact that the O line depends on the rate of interest thus

> "... evidently does not alter the principles by which the slope of the *M* line is determined. The *M* line still rolls around an *O* line, even if that curve changes a little as it rolls." (1930: 279)

FISHER supports his conclusion also in the context of his algebraic presentation of the second approximation (1907: 401-2, 1930: 310n10). The introduction of the dependence of the range of choice on the rate of interest only introduces the rates of interest into each of the equations representing an opportunity line, without, however, affecting either the number of equations or the number of unknowns. It thus "does not affect the determinateness of the problem" (1907: 402, 1930: 310n10).[148]

Note that, contrary to FISHER's assertion (1907: 93, quoted in Chapter 3 above), his explanation of the determination of the rate of interest has left us so far without indication why the rate of interest should generally be positive.[149] It should not go unnoticed, however, that he follows his second approximation with an extended discussion of stylized "Classes of Options" (1907: 178-97) which, although inserted for a different objective,[150] will be seen to be not entirely irrelevant to the point in question. We shall here pick out four "classes of options" for closer scrutiny. In the first, FISHER envisages the case of "a desert island on which some sailors are shipwrecked and left each with 1000 pounds of hardtack and no prospect of ever improving their lot" (1907: 181). He concludes that in this case, since the rate of return on sacrifice would be zero, the rate of interest in terms of hardtack would necessarily also be zero:

> "A little reflection will show that in such a community the rate of interest in terms of hardtack would necessarily be zero. For, by hypothesis, the sacrifice of one pound of hardtack unconsumed from this year's income can only result in an equal increase in the income of future years. Therefore the *rate of return on sacrifice* is zero. Since this rate must equal the rates of preference and the rate of interest, these rates must be zero also." (1907: 181)[151]

In the second class of options, which is to exemplify the "effect of the slowness of Nature on interest" (1907: xvi, cf. 185-6), the example is slightly modified. It is now envisaged that the total amount of consumption is again fixed and foreknown, but that portions of it are forthcoming at certain intervals. It is "as though the hardtack had in some way been stored in a series of storehouses, each provided with a time lock arranged to open at a certain date. There is a certain amount of income, but it is only available at intervals." (1907: 185) In this case, so FISHER, "unless the time locks are timed to open as fast (or even faster, I.P.) as the castaways would have chosen of themselves to eat their stores" (ibid.), the rate of interest would be positive:

> "We see, therefore, that in order that a positive rate of interest shall emerge, it is only necessary that income shall sufficiently hold back its flow. ... In fact, if we were asked to state in a word why there is interest, we should reply, because nature is slow and keeps man waiting." (1907: 186)

---

148 That FISHER is exclusively concerned with mathematical determinateness is also apparent in his dealing with another circularity problem (see 1907: 147-9).

149 Recall that we have judged unsatisfactory FISHER's lapidary statement that interest is positive simply because intertemporal statements are expressed in terms of money which "possesses durability, and can be hoarded without loss" (1907: 93, quoted in Chapter 3 above).

150 His objective is "to present a full view of what is meant by 'optional employments of capital'" (1907: 178).

151 FISHER implicitly assumes that hardtack can be stored without cost or decay.

Note that the result of FISHER's second class of options indicates that the rate of interest need not necessarily be equal to the marginal rate of return on sacrifice, which is again equal to zero. Next, FISHER turns to elucidate the "effect of the productivity of Nature on interest" (1907: xvi, cf. 186-7) by positing a "class of options... in which, if present income is sacrificed for the sake of future income, the amount of the latter secured thereby is greater than that of the former sacrificed" (1907: 186). If this is the case throughout, and FISHER leaves no doubt he believes it is in practice (cf. 1907: 186-7), then the individual will postpone present consumption until a positive rate of interest emerges. From this, FISHER concludes that

> "... while the slowness of Nature is a sufficient cause for interest, her productivity is an additional cause. ... Nature offers man, as one of her optional income-streams, the possibility of great future abundance at trifling present sacrifice. This option acts as a bribe to man to sacrifice present income for future, and this tends to make present income scarce and future income abundant and hence also to create in his mind a preference for a unit of present over a unit of future income." (1907: 186-7)

FISHER does not, in this context, explicitly reassert any conformity of the rate of interest with the marginal rate of return on sacrifice. But he does so implicitly, as becomes clear from the following fourth class of options. In this class, he analyzses a case in which the goods considered "deteriorate at the foreknown rate of 50 per cent per annum" (1907: 187). He concludes that

> "(i)n this case, the rate of interest would be necessarily *minus* 50 per cent per annum." (1907: 187)

By parallel reasoning, if income augments at a foreknown rate of 50 per cent, the rate of interest would likewise be *plus* 50 per cent.

We have thus seen how far removed FISHER is from completely discounting the role played by technical productivity conditions in the explanation of either the determination of the size or the positivity of the sign of the rate of interest. Indeed, as FISHER later emphasizes in response to SEAGER's endictments, the reconstruction of the technical element in the explanation of interest had been "my chief reason in writing the *Rate of Interest*" (1913: 610).[152],[153] And yet, we have

---

152 "The fact is that my chief reason in writing the *Rate of Interest* at all arose from the belief that Böhm-Bawerk and others had failed to discover the true way in which the 'technique of production' enters into the determination of the rate of interest. Believing the technical link in previous explanations unsound, and realizing ... the absolute necessity of such a link, I set myself the task of finding it. In the desirability of this I emphatically agree with Böhm-Bawerk." (1913: 610)

153 FISHER says in the same article that "it was through mathematics that I saw the nature and importance of productivity in relation to interest" (1913: 612). Here the reference is to his algebraic method: "There is a principle of mathematics that says that a problem is determinate only when the number of independent determining conditions are equal to the number of unknown quantities to be determined ... . Whatever sins of ommission are open to the

seen that FISHER regarded himself a follower of BÖHM-BAWERK's "agio theory" - the theory that "finds the essence of the rate of interest in the agio or premium of present goods when exchanged for future goods" (1907: 53, quoted this chapter above). It is true, he only finds this "the natural and proper starting-point for any rational discussion of the subject" (ibid.), a view which he emphasizes almost programmatically in his "Preface:"

> "The difficult problem is not whether the rate of interest *is* an agio, or premium, for of this there can be no question, but upon what does this agio depend and in what manner?" (1907: vii)

And yet, the very opening line of *The Rate of Interest* reads:

> "If the theory to be presented in this book is correct, the rate of interest in any community is an index of the preference, in that community, for a dollar of present over a dollar of future income." (1907: 3)

indicating that the view in question, rather than being a mere starting-point of, is the central insight to be gained *from* his analysis of interest. And again, in introducing the more positive sections of his book he writes, drawing the explicit analogy to the theory of prices:

> "Just as in the ordinary theory of prices the ratio of exchange of any two articles is based on a psychological or subjective element, - their comparative marginal utility, - so in the theory of interest the rate of interest, or the premium in the exchange of present and future goods, is based on a subjective prototype; namely, the preference for present over future goods. This 'time-preference' is the central fact in the theory of interest." (1907: 88)[154]

That this is indeed FISHER's position becomes more amply apparent in his (1911) article on "The 'Impatience Theory' of Interest," which is reprinted almost verbatim in his *Elementary Principles of Economics* textbook (1912). Physical productivity is here discarded as having "no power whatever to create interest" (1911: 386) so that "it is futile to derive the rate of interest from the productivity of capital" (1912: 368). The notion of time preference is replaced by that of "impatience" which "seems to be the only one expressing accurately and in a single word, the real basis of interest" (1911: 386).[155] Although he claims that this

---

mathematical economist, the particular sin of omission (such as overlooking one of the necessary conditions determining the rate of interest) is scarcely open to him at all." (1913: 613) In *The Rate of Interest*, we find a similar reference to the geometric method: "The geometrical method enables them (those conversant with the mathematical tongue, I.P.) to form a mental picture, clearer than would otherwise be possible, of the various factors at work, and especially of the manner in which the objective or 'technical' conditions ... coöperate with the subjective conditions which influence the rate of interest. It was, in fact, only through the geometrical representation that the writer was first enabled to grasp the significance of the 'effective range of choice' in its general bearings. If the rôle of the curve is grasped, the most difficult part of the theory of interest is mastered." (1907: 415)

154 There is a general reference at this point to FETTER (1904).

155 "In my own book, "The Rate of Interest," ... the clumsier and less self- ex-planatory term "time-preference" was employed instead. The proposal to employ the term "impatience" is

terminological change "does not in the least affect the principles involved," he now writes, directly contradicting his own earlier assertions to the contrary (cf. Chapter 4 above):

> "Impatience is a fundamental attribute of human nature. As long as people like to have things today rather than tomorrow, there will be a rate of interest. *Interest is, as it were, impatience crystallized into a market rate.*" (1911: 387)[156]

And again:

> "*The essence of interest is impatience*, the desire to obtain gratifications earlier than we can get them, the preference for present over future goods. It is a fundamental attribute of human nature." (1912: 371, e.a.)

Moreover, he confines his presentation of the determination of the rate of interest basically to his first approximation, culminating in the characteristic conclusion that

> "(t)he rate of interest is simply the rate of impatience, upon which the whole community may concur in order that the market of loans will be cleared." (1911: 386; cf. 1912: 398-9)

In both publications mention of "optional uses to which a man may put his capital" (1912: 400) or "marginal rates of return on sacrifice" (1911: 398) is merely appended without being allowed to detract in any way from the conclusions reached as to the ultimate "cause" or "essence" of interest.

In respone to SEAGER's (1912) criticism of the subjectivist leaning of his impatience theory, FISHER, of course, stressed these latter passages which, as he said, he had merely appended in what was to be an elementary text because of the complexity and controversiality of the questions involved. For the rest, he apologized for not having made his position clearer (1913: 617). In his *Theory of Interest* (1930) many controversial passages are altered to explicitly admit the productivity element (e.g. 1930: 61-2; cf. 1907: 88) which also figures in the subtitle "... As Determined by Impatience To Spend Income and Opportunity To Invest It."

---

here made for the first time." (1911: 387) The Section in question carries the title "Human Impatience the true Basis of Interest" (1911: 386), its corresponding section in the *Principles* "Impatience the Source of Interest" (1912: 371).

156 In his later *Theory of Interest* (1930), although now dedicating a full paragraph to the fact that "Time Preference May be Negative", FISHER judges the statement that a positive rate of time preference is a fundamental attribute of human nature "too narrow" instead of simply calling it "false." Referring to situations "representing small *future* and large *present* income," he writes: "At such income positions the rate of time preference would be negative. It is sometimes said that it is a fundamental attribute of human nature to prefer a dinner or a dollar this year to a dinner or a dollar next year, but this statement is evidently too narrow. Unconsciously it confines the view to regions of the income map where present income is relatively small and future income relatively large." (1930: 248)

Unfortunately, FISHER does not reflect the incongruities of his position. Such reflection, it is here argued, might have revealed that FISHER's "impatience theory of interest" comprised not only an explanation of the determination of the size and of the positivity of the sign of the rate of interest, but also an underlying explanation of the essence of interest. This latter aspect, it has been argued, can also be discerned in BÖHM-BAWERK's "agio theory." It is this aspect, that should be identified as the exclusive concern of the Austrian subjectivist theory of interest.

Literature

ALBERT, Hans (1988): "Hermeneutics and Economics. A Criticism of Hermeneutical Thinking in Economics," in *Kyklos* 41, 573-602.

ARVIDSSON, Guy (1953): "On rätans grunder," in Economisk Tidskrift; translated by Alan WILLIAMS as "On the Reasons for the Rate of Interest," in *International Economic Papers* 6 (1956), 23-33.

ATLANTIC ECONOMIC JOURNAL (ed. 1978): *Carl Menger's Contribution to Economics*, Special Issue, Sept 1978.

BAIRD, Charles W. (1982): *Prices and Markets. Intermediate Microeconomics*, St. Paul: West Publishing.

BARRY, Norman P. (1983): "Review Article: The New Liberalism," in *British Journal of Political Science* 13, 93-123.

BECKER, O. and R. RICHTER (eds. 1975): *Dynamische Wirtschaftsanalyse*, Tübingen: Mohr.

BELL, John F. (1953): *A History of Economic Thought*, New York.

BELL, Daniel and Irving KRISTOL (eds. 1981): *The Crisis in Economic Theory*, New York: Basic Books.

BERNHOLZ, Peter (1971): "Superiority of Roundabout Processes and Positive Rate of Interest. A Simple Model of Capital and Growth," in *Kyklos* 24, 687-721.

BLOCK, Walter and Llewellyn H. ROCKWELL (eds. 1988): *Man, Economy, and Liberty. Essays in Honor of Murray N. Rothbard*, Auburn (Alabama): Ludwig von Mises Institute.

BÖHM-BAWERK, Eugen von (1881): *Rechte und Verhältnisse vom Standpunkte der volkswirthschaftlichen Güterlehre*, Innsbruck: Wagnersche Universitätsbuchhandlung; reprinted in BÖHM-BAWERK (1924-1926), I: 1-126; translated by George D. HUNCKE as "Whether Legal Rights and Relationships are Economic Goods," in BÖHM-BAWERK (1962), 25-138.

BÖHM-BAWERK, Eugen von (1884-1889): *Kapital und Kapitalzins*, 1st ed., 2 vols., Innsbruck: Wagner; 4th ed., 3 vols, Jena: Fischer, 1921; translation of 1st ed. by William SMART, 2 vols., New York: Kelley, 1890-1891; translation of 4th ed. by George D. HUNCKE and Hans F. SENNHOLZ under the title *Capital and Interest*, 3 vols., South Holl. (Ill.): Libertarian Press 1959.

BÖHM-BAWERK, Eugen von (1896): "Zum Abschluss des Marxschen Systems," in *Staatswissenschaftliche Arbeiten - Festgaben für Karl Knies zur Fünfundsiebzigsten Wiederkehr*, Berlin: Haering, 85-205; translated by Alice MACDONALD as "Carl Marx and the Close of his System," New York: Macmillan 1898; reprinted New York: Kelley 1949; reprinted as "Unresolved Contradiction of the Marxian Economic System," in *Shorter Classics of Eugen von Böhm-Bawerk*, South Holland, Ill.: Libertarian Press, 201-302.

BÖHM-BAWERK, Eugen von (1900): *Einige Strittige Fragen der Capitalstheorie*, Wien etc.: Braumüller.

BÖHM-BAWERK, Eugen von (1911): "Zins," in *Handwörterbuch der Staatswissenschaften*, vol. 8, 1004-1017; reprinted in BÖHM-BAWERK (1924-1926), II: 21-51.

BÖHM-BAWERK, Eugen von (1924-1926): *Gesammelte Schriften*, 2 vols., Wien: Hölder, Pichler, Tempski.

BÖHM-BAWERK, Eugen von (1962): *Shorter Classics of Eugen von Böhm-Bawerk*, South Holland (Ill.): Libertarian Press. (A projected second volume of the *Shorter Classics* was never published.)

BORTKIEWICZ, Ladislaus von (1906): "Der Kardinalfehler der Böhm-Bawerkschen Zinstheorie," in *Schmoller's Jahrbücher*, 30.

BROWN, Harry G. (1913): "The Marginal Productivity Versus the Impatience Theory of Interest," in *Quarterly Journal of Economics* XXVII, 630-50.

BROWN, Harry G. (1914): "The Discount Versus the Cost of Production Theory of Capital Valuation," in *American Economic Review* 4, 340-9.

BURMEISTER, Edwin (1974): "Synthesizing the Neo-Austrian and Alternative Approaches to Capital Theory: A Survey," in *Journal of Economic Literature* 12, 413-456.

CONARD, Joseph W. (1959): *An Introduction to the Theory of Interest*, Berkeley etc., University of California Press.

DOLAN, Edwin G. (ed. 1976): *The Foundations of Modern Austrian Economics*, Kansas City: Sheed & Ward.

DOLAN, Edwin G. (1976): "Austrian Economics as Extraordinary Science," in DOLAN (ed. 1976), 3-15.

DORFMAN, Joseph (1949): *The Economic Mind in American Civilization*, 5 vols., New York: Viking Press.

EATWELL, John, Murray MILGATE, and Peter NEWMAN (eds. 1987): *The New Palgrave. A Dictionary in Economics*, 4 vols., London: Macmillan.

ENDRES, Alfred M. (1987): "The Origins of Böhm-Bawerk's Greatest Error: Theoretical Points of Separation from Menger," in *Zeitschrift für die gesamte Staatswissenschaft* (*Journal of Institutional and Theoretical Economics*) 143, 291-309

FABER, Malte (1979): *Introduction to Modern Austrian Capital Theory*, Berlin etc.: Springer.

FABER, Malte (ed. 1986): *Studies in Austrian Capital Theory. Investment, and Time*, Berlin etc.: Springer.

FABER, Malte (1986): "On the Development of Austrian Capital Theory," in FABER (ed. 1986), 12-43.

FEHL, Ulrich (1973): *Produktionsfunktion und Produktionsperiode. Eine Auseinandersetzung mit dem Grundbegriff der temporalen Kapitaltheorie*, Göttingen: Vandenhoeck & Ruprecht.

FEHL, Ulrich (1976): "Die durchschnittliche Produktionsperiode als Grundbegriff der temporalen Kapitaltheorie," in Zeitschrift für Wirtschafts- und Sozialwissenschaften 95, 135-70.

FETTER, Frank A. (1894): *Versuch einer Bevölkerungslehre ausgehend von einer Kritik des Malthusschen Bevölkerungsprinzips*, Dissertation, Jena: Fischer.

FETTER, Frank A. (1900): "Recent Discussion of the Capital Concept," in *Quarterly Journal of Economics* 15, 1-45; reprinted in FETTER (1977), 33-73.

FETTER, Frank A. (1901): "The Next Decade of Economic Theory," in *Papers and Proceedings of the Thirteenth Meeting of the American Economic Association* 2; reprinted in FETTER (1977), 74-83.

FETTER, Frank A. (1902): Review of BÖHM-BAWERK's *Einige strittige Fragen der Capitalstheorie*, in *Political Science Quarterly* 17; reprinted in FETTER (1977), 87-91.

FETTER, Frank A. (1902a): "The 'Roundabout Process' in the Interest Theory," in *Quarterly Journal of Economics* 17, 163-80; reprinted in FETTER (1977), 172-91.

FETTER, Frank A. (1904): *The Principles of Economics*, New York: The Century Co..

FETTER, Frank A. (1904a): "The Relations between Rent and Interest," in *Papers and Proceedings of the Sixteenth Annual Meeting of the American Economic Association* 5; reprinted in FETTER (1977), 192-221.

FETTER, Frank A. (1914): "Interest Theories, Old and New," in *American Economic Review* 4; reprinted in FETTER (1977), 226-55.

FETTER, Frank A. (1914a): "Capitalization versus Productivity. A Rejoinder," in *American Economic Review* 5; reprinted in FETTER (1977), 192-221.

FETTER, Frank A. (1915): *Economics*, vol. 1: *Economic Principles*, New York: The Century Co..

FETTER, Frank A. (1930-5): "Capital," in *Encyclopedia of the Social Sciences*; reprinted in FETTER (1977), 143-50.

FETTER, Frank A. (1930-5a): "Rent," in *Encyclopedia of the Social Sciences*, reprinted in FETTER (1977), 366-73.

FETTER, Frank A. (1937): "Reformulation of the Concepts of Capital and Income in Economics and Accounting," in *Accounting Review* 12; reprinted in FETTER (1977), 151-70.

FETTER, Frank A. (1977): *Capital, Interest, and Rent. Essays in the Theory of Distribution*, edited with an Introduction by Murray N. ROTHBARD, Kansas City: Sheed Andrews and McMeel (Universal Press).

FETTER, Frank A.: see also MAYER et al. (1927-1932).

FISHER, Irving (1892): "Mathematical Investigations in the Theory of Value and Prices," in *Transcations of Conneticut Academy*, New Haven.

FISHER, Irving (1906): *The Nature of Capital and Income*, New York: Macmillan.

FISHER, Irving (1907): *The Rate of Interest*, New York: Macmillan

FISHER, Irving (1911): "The Impatience Theory of Interest," in *Scientia, Rivista di scienza, International Review of Scientific Synthesis* IX, 380-401.

FISHER, Irving (1912): *Elementary Principles of Economics*, New York: Macmillan.

FISHER, Irving (1913): "The Impatience Theory of Interest," in *American Economic Review* 3, 610-18.

FISHER, Irving (1930): *The Theory of Interest*, New York: Macmillan.

GADAMER, Hans-Georg (1965): *Wahrheit und Methode. Grundzüge einer philosophischen Hermeneutik*, Tübingen: Mohr; translated as *Truth and Method. Principles of Philosophical Hermeneutics*.

GARRISON, Roger W. (1978): "Austrian Macroeconomics. A Diagrammatical Exposition," in SPADARO (ed. 1978), 167-204.

GARRISON, Roger W. (1979): "In Defense of the Misesian Theory of Interest," in *Journal for Libertarian Studies* 3, 141-50.

GARRISON, Roger W. (1979a): "Waiting in Vienna," in RIZZO (ed. 1979), 215-26.

GARRISON, Roger W. (1980): Review of FABER (1979), in *Austrian Economics Newsletter* 2 (no. 3) , pp. 5 and 11.

GARRISON, Roger W. (1985): "A Subjectivist View of a Capital-Using Economy," in O'DRISCOLL et al. (1985), 160-87.

GARRISON, Roger W. (1988): "Professor Rothbard and the Theory of Interest," in BLOCK et al. (eds. 1988), 44-55.

GRAM, Harvey and Vivian C. WALSH (1980): *Classical and Neoclassical Theories of General Equilibrium. Historical Origins and Mathematical Structure*, New York etc.: Oxford University Press.

GREAVES, Percy L. Jr. (1974): *Mises Made Easier. A Glossary for Ludwig von Mises' Human Action*, Dobbs Ferry (N.Y.): Free Market Books.

GREENWALD, Douglas (ed. 1982): *Encyclopedia of Economics*, New York: McGraw-Hill.

GRINDER, Walter E. (1977): "In Pursuit of the Subjective Paradigm," in LACHMANN (1977), 3-24.

HARCOURT, Geoffrey C. and N. F. LAING (eds. 1971): *Capital and Growth*, Hammondsworth: Penguin.

HAUSMAN, Daniel M. (1981): *Capital, Profits, and Prices. An Essay in the Philosophy of Economics*, New York: Columbia University Press.

HAYEK, Friedrich A. von (1931): *Prices and Production*, London: Routledge.

HAYEK, Friedrich A. von (1933): *Monetary Theory and the Trade Cycle*, London: Cape.

HAYEK, Friedrich A. von (1939): *Profits, Interest, and Investment, and Other Essays on the Theory of Industrian Fluctuations*, London: Routledge.

HAYEK, Friedrich A. von (1945): "Time-Preference and Productivity. A Reconsideration," in *Economica* N.S. 12, 22-5.

HAYEK, Friedrich A. von (1955): *The Counter-revolution of Science. Studies on the Abuse of Reason*, Glencoe Ill.: Free Press.

HENNINGS, Klaus H. (1972): *The Austrian Theory of Value and Capital. Studies in the Life and Work of Eugen von Böhm-Bawerk*, Ph.D. dissertation, Oxford: Ruffield College.

HERBENER, Jeffrey M. (ed. 1993): *The Meaning of Ludwig von Mises. Contributions in Economics, Sociology, Epistemology, and Political Philosophy*, Norwell (Mass.): Kluwer Academic Publishers.

HICKS, John R. (1965): *Capital and Growth*, Oxford: Clarendon Press.

HICKS, John R. (1967): *Critical Essays in Monetary Theory*, Oxford: Clarendon Press.

HICKS, John R. (1967a): "The Hayek Story," in HICKS (1967), 203-15.

HICKS, John R. (1973): *Capital and Time. A Neo-Austrian Theory*, Oxford: Clarendon Press.

HICKS, John R. (1973a): "The Austrian Theory of Capital and its Rebirth in Modern Economics," in HICKS and WEBER (eds. 1973), 190-206.

HICKS, John R. (1979): "Is Interest the Price of a Factor of Production?" in RIZZO (ed. 1979), 51-63; reprinted in HICKS (1983), vol. 3.

HICKS, John R. (1983): *Classics and Modern. Essays on Economic Theory*, 3 vols., Oxford: Basil Blackwell.

HICKS, John R. and Wilhelm WEBER (eds. 1973): *Carl Menger and the Austrian School of Economics*, Oxford: Clarendon Press.

HOXIE, Robert F. (1905): "Fetter's Theory of Value," in *Quarterly Journal of Economics* 19, 210-30.

HUTCHISON, Terence W. (1973): "Some Themes from Investigations into Method," in HICKS et al. (eds. 1973), 15-37.

JAFFÉ, William (ed. 1965): *Correspondence of Léon Walras and Related Papers*, 3 vols., Amsterdam: North Holland.

JAKSCH, Hans J. (1975): "Die Mehrergiebigkeit längerer Produktionsumwege in einem linearen Vielsektorenmodell," in *Zeitschrift für die gesamte Staatswissenschaft* 131, 92-105.

JAKSCH, Hans J. (1975a): "Effizienz und Minderschätzung künftiger Bedürfnisse in einem linearen Vielsektorenmodell," in BECKER and RICHTER (eds. 1975), 87-104.

JEVONS, William S. (1870): *Theory of Political Economy*, London: Macmillan.

KALDOR, Nicholas (1937): "Annual Survey of Economic Theory: The Recent Controversy on the Theory of Capital," in *Econometrica* 5, 201-33.

KAUDER, Emil (1957): "Intellectual and Political Roots of the Older Austrian School," in *Zeitschrift für Nationalökonomie* (*Journal of Economics*) 17, 411-25.

KAUDER, Emil (1965): *A History of Marginal Utility Theory*, Princeton: Princeton University Press.

KIRZNER, Israel M. (1976): "Ludwig von Mises and the Theory of Interest," in MOSS (ed. 1976), 51-66.

KIRZNER, Israel M. (1976a): "On the Method of Austrian Economics," in DOLAN (ed. 1976), 40-51.

KIRZNER, Israel M. (1976b): "Philosophical and Ethical Implications of Austrian Economics," in DOLAN (ed. 1976), 75-88.

KIRZNER, Israel M. (1980): Review of FETTER (1977), in *Austrian Economics Newsletter* 2, 8-9.

KIRZNER, Israel M. (1981): "The 'Austrian' Perspective on the Crisis," in BELL and KRISTOL (eds. 1981), 111-22.

KIRZNER, Israel M. (ed. 1982): *Method, Process, and Austrian Economics. Essays in Honor of Ludwig von Mises*, Lexington etc.: Lexington Books.

KIRZNER, Israel M. (1983): The Pure Time Preference Theory of Interest. A Postscript to the Grand Debate," unpublished manuscript, New York University.

KIRZNER, Israel M. (1983a): Review of HAUSMAN (1981), in *International Philosophical Quarterly*, 220-2.

KIRZNER, Israel M. (ed. 1986): *Subjectivism, Intelligibility, and Economic Understanding. Essays in Honor of Ludwig M. Lachmann on his Eightieth Birthday*, New York: New York University Press.

KIRZNER, Israel M (1987): "Austrian School of Economics," in EATWELL et al. (eds. 1987), 145-51.

KIRZNER, Israel M. (1993): "The Pure Time-Preference Theory of Interest. An Attempt at Clarification," in HERBENER (ed. 1993), 166-92.

KNIGHT, Frank H. (1941): "Professor Mises and the Theory of Capital," in *Economica* N.S. 8, 409-27.

KOOPMANS, Tjalling C. (1960): "Stationary Ordinal Utility and Impatience," in *Econometrica* 28, 287-309.

KRAUS, Oskar (1905): "Die Aristotelische Werttheorie in ihren Beziehungen zu den Lehren der modernen Psychologenschule," in *Zeitschrift für die gesamte Staatswissenschaft* 61.

KRISTOL, Irving: see BELL and KRISTOL (eds. 1981).

LACHMANN, Ludwig M. (1971): *The Legacy of Max Weber*, Berkeley: Glendessary Press; translated into German as *Drei Essays über Max Webers geistiges Vermächtnis*, Tübingen: Mohr, 1973.

LACHMANN, Ludwig M. (1973): "Sir John Hicks as a Neo-Austrian," in South African Journal of Economics 41: 195-207; reprinted in LACHMANN (1977), 251-66.

LACHMANN, Ludwig M. (1976): "On Austrian Capital Theory," in DOLAN (ed. 1976), 145-51.

LACHMANN, Ludwig M. (1977): *Capital, Expectations, and the Market Process. Essays on the Theory of the Market Economy*, Kansas City: Sheed Andrews and McMeel.

LACHMANN, Ludwig M. (1977a): "Austrian Economics in the Present Crisis of Economic Thought," in LACHMANN (1977), 25-41.

LACHMANN, Ludwig M. (1982): "The Salvage of Ideas. Problems of the Revival of Austrian Economic Thought," in *Zeitschrift für die gesamte Staatswissenschaft (Journal of Institutional and Theoretical Economics)* 138, 629-45.

LAING, N. F.: see HARCOURT and LAING (eds. 1971).

LANDRY, Adolphe (1904): *L'intérêt du capital*, Paris: Giard & Brière.

LAUNHARDT, Wilhelm (1885): *Mathematische Begründung der Volkswirtschaftslehre*, Leipzig.

LAVOIE, Don (1985): *Rivalry and Central Planning. The Socialist Calculation Debate Reconsidered*, Cambridge, etc.: Cambridge University Press.

LAVOIE, Don (1986): "Euclideanism versus Hermeneutics. A Reinterpretation of Misesian Apriorism," in KIRZNER (ed. 1986), 192-210.

LITTLECHILD, Stephen C. and G. OWEN (1980): "An Austrian Model of the Entrepreneurial Market Process," in *Journal of Economic Theory* 23, 361-79.

LITTLECHILD, Stephen C. (ed. 1990): *Austrian Economics*, 3 vols., Aldershot: Elgar.

LUTZ, Friedrich A. (1967): *Zinstheorie*, 2nd ed., Tübingen: Mohr.

MACHLUP, Fritz (1982): "Austrian Economics," in GREENWALD (ed. 1982).

MARSHALL, Alfred (1889): *Principles of Economics*, London: Macmillan; 8th ed. London: Macmillan 1930.

MAYER, Hans, Richard REISCH, and Frank A. FETTER (eds. 1927-1932): *Die Wirtschaftstheorie der Gegenwart*, 4 vols., Vienna: Springer.

MAYER, Hans (1932): "Der Erkenntniswert der funktionellen Preistheorien," in MAYER et al. (eds. 1927-1932), vol. II, 147-239b.

MCCLOSKEY, Donald N. (1983): "The Rethoric of Economics," in *Journal of Economic Literature* XXI, 481-517.

MCCLOSKEY, Donald N. (1985): *The Rethoric of Economics*, Madison: University of Wisconsin Press.

MENGER, Carl (1871): *Grundsätze der Volkswirtschaftslehre*, Vienna: Braumüller; reprinted as vol. I of *The Collected Works of Carl Menger*, with an Introduction by Friedrich A. von HAYEK, London: London School of Economics, 1935; reprinted, with a revised Introduction by Friedrich A. von HAYEK, Tübingen: Mohr, 1968; translated by James DINGWALL and Bert F. HOSELITZ as *Principles of Economics*, with an Introduction by Frank H. KNIGHT, Glencoe, Ill.: Libertarian Press, 1950; reprinted with an Introduction by Friedrich A. von HAYEK, New York: New York University Press, 1981.

MENGER, Carl (1883): *Untersuchungen über die Methode der Socialwissenschaften und der Politischen Oekonomie insbesondere*, Leipzig: Duncker und Humblot; reprinted as vol. II of *The Collected Works of Carl Menger*, London: London School of Economics, 1935; translated by Francis J. NOCK as *Problems of Economics and Sociology*, Urbana: University of Illinois Press, 1963; reprinted as *Investigations into the Method of the Social Sciences with Special Reference to Economics*, with an Introduction by Lawrence H. WHITE, New York: New York University Press, 1985.

MENGER, Carl (1888): "Zur Theorie des Kapitals," in *Conrads Jahrbücher für Nationalökonomie und Statistik* 17, 135-8; reprinted in vol. III of *The Collected Works of Carl Menger*, London: London School of Economics 1935; reprinted in MENGER, Carl: *Gesammelte Werke*, vol. III, Tübingen: Mohr 1968, 1-49.

MENGER, Carl (1923): *Grundsätze der Volkswirtschaftslehre*, second (posthumous) edition, edited by Karl MENGER, with a Preface by Richard SCHÜLLER, Vienna: Hölder, Pichler, Tempsky.

MENGER, Karl (1923): "Vorwort des Herausgebers," in Carl MENGER (1923), V-XXII.

MISES, Ludwig von (1912): *Theorie des Geldes und der Umlaufmittel*, München: Duncker & Humblot; 2nd ed., München: Duncker und Humblot 1924; 2nd ed. translated under the title *The Theory of Money and Credit* by H. E. BATSON, New Haven: Yale University Press 1959.

MISES, Ludwig von (1940): *Nationalökonomie. Theorie des Handelns und Wirtschaftens*, Geneva: Editions Union.

MISES, Ludwig von (1943): "'Elastic Expectations' and the Austrian Theory of the Trade Cycle," in *Economica* 10, 251-2.

MISES, Ludwig von (1949): *Human Action*, New Haven: Yale University Press.

MISES, Ludwig von (1940/1974): "A Critique of Böhm-Bawerk's Reasoning in Support of his Time Preference Theory," translation of MISES (1940: 439-44) by Bettina Bien GREAVES, in GREAVES (1974), 150-7.

MITCHELL, Wesley C. (1967-1969): *Types of Economic Theory. From Mercantilism to Institutionalism*, edited with an Introduction by Joseph DORFMAN, 2 vols., New York: Kelley.

MIXTER, Charles W. (1897): "A Forerunner of Böhm-Bawerk," in *Quarterly Journal of Economics* 11, 161-90.

MOLDOVSKY, Naomi (1982): Review of FABER (1979), in *Economic Record* 58, 295-7.

MOSS, Laurence S. (ed. 1976): *The Economics of Ludwig von Mises. Towards a Critical Reappraisal*, Kansas City: Sheed and Ward.

MOSS, Laurence S. (1978): "The Emergence of Interest in a Pure Exchange Economy: Notes on a Theorem Attributed to Ludwig von Mises," in SPADARO (ed. 1978), 157-66.

MOSS, Laurence S. (1980): Review of FABER (1979), in *Journal of Economic Literature* 18, 1096-8.

MOSS, Laurence S. and Karen I. VAUGHN (1982): "Modern Böhm-Bawerkian Capital Theory and Modern Austrian Economics: A Proposed Reconciliation," paper presented at the History of Economic Society Meeting, unpublished manuscript.

NELL, Edward J. (1967): "Theories of Growth and Theories of Value," in *Economic Theory and Cultural Change* XVI, 15-26; reprinted in HARCOURT and LAING (eds. 1971), 196-210.

NELL, Edward J. (1981): "Value and Capital in Marxian Economics," in BELL and KRISTOL (eds. 1981), 174-200.

NORDHAUS, William D.: see SAMUELSON and NORDHAUS (1985).

O'DRISCOLL, Gerald P. (1977): "*Economics as a Coordination Problem. The Contributions of F. A. von Hayek*, Kansas City: Sheed Andrews and McMeel.

O'DRISCOLL, Gerald P. (1979): "The Pure Time Preference Theory of Interest Rate Determination," unpublished manuscript, Iowa State University. (Revised version of a paper of the same title presented at the History of Economics Society Meeting, Toronto 1978.)

O'DRISCOLL, Gerald P. (1980): "Frank A. Fetter and 'Austrian Business Cycle Theory," in *History of Political Economy* 12, 542-57.

O'DRISCOLL, Gerald P. and Mario J. RIZZO (1985): *The Economics of Time and Ignorance*, Oxford etc.: Basil Blackwell.

OROSEL, Gerhard O. (1979): "A Reformulation of the Austrian Theory of Capital and its Application to the Debate on Reswitching and Related Paradoxa," in Zeitschrift für Nationalökonomie 39, 1-31.

OWEN, G.: see LITTLECHILD and OWEN (1980).

PASINETTI, Luigi L. (1969): "Switches of Technique and the Rate of Return in Capital Theory," in *Economic Journal* 79, 508-25 and 529-31; reprinted in HARCOURT and LAING (eds. 1971).

PELLENGAHR, Ingo (1984): "The Pure Time-Preference Theory of Interest. A Critique," Austrian Colloquium Discussion Paper (mimeographed), New York University.

PELLENGAHR, Ingo (1986): "Austrian vs. Austrians I: A Subjectivist View of Interest," in FABER (ed. 1986), 60-77.

PELLENGAHR, Ingo (1986a): "Austrian vs. Austrians II: Functionalist vs. Essentialist Theories of Interest," in FABER (ed. 1986), 78-95.

PIERSON, Nicolas G. (1899): "Literaturüberblick," in *De Economist*.

RAE, John (1834): *Statement of some New Principles on the Subject of Political Economy, exposing the Fallacies of the System of Free Trade, and of some other Doctrines maintained in the 'Wealth of Nations,'"* Boston: Hilliard, Gray & Co..

REEKIE, Duncan W. (1984): *Markets, Entrepreneurs, and Liberty. An Austrian View of Capitalism*, Brighton: Wheatsheaf Books.

REETZ, Norbert (1971): *Produktionsfunktion und Produktionsperiode. Kritische Darstellung des Produktionsperiodenmodells Böhm-Bawerkschen Typs und Vergleich mit der neoklassischen Wachstumstheorie*, Göttingen: Schwartz.

REETZ, Norbert (1976): *Zeitlicher Produktionsablauf und Kapitalakkumulation*, Göttingen: Schwartz.

REETZ, Norbert (1984): "Österreichische Kapitaltheorie, neoklassisches Wachstum und Konjunktur," in Schweizerische Zeitschrift für Volkswirtschaft und Statistik 120, 1-30.

REISCH, Richard: see MAYER et al. (eds. 1927-1932).

REISS, Winfried (1979): "Substitution in a Neo-Austrian Model of Capital," in *Zeitschrift für Nationalökonomie* 39, 33-52.

REISS, Winfried (1981): *Umwegproduktion und Positivität des Zinses. Eine neo-österreichische Analyse*, Berlin: Duncker & Humblot.

RICHTER, G.: see BECKER and RICHTER (eds. 1975).

RIZZO, Mario J. (ed. 1979): *Time, Uncertainty, and Disequilibrium, Exploration of Austrian Themes*, Lexington: Lexington Books.

RIZZO, Mario J.: see also O'DRISCOLL and RIZZO (1985).

ROBBINS, Lionel (1932): *The Nature and Significance of Economic Science*, London: Macmillan.

ROSCHER, Wilhelm (1854): *Grundlagen der Nationalökonomie*, Stuttgart etc.: Cotta.

ROTHBARD, Murray N. (1957): "In Defense of Extreme Apriorism," in *Southern Economic Lournal* 23, 315-8.

ROTHBARD, Murray N. (1962): *Man, Economy, and State*, 2 vols.; republished in one volume, Los Angeles: Nash, 1970.

ROTHBARD, Murray N. (1976): "Praxeology: The Methodology of Austrian Economics," in *Dolan* (ed. 1976), 19-39.

ROTHBARD, Murray N.: (1976a): "Praxeology, Value Judgements, and Public Policy," in DOLAN (ed. 1976), 89-111.

ROTHBARD, Murray N. (1977): "Preface," in FETTER (1977).

ROTHBARD, Murray N. (1977a): "Introduction," in FETTER (1977), 1-24; reprinted in LITTLECHILD (ed. 1990), II: 108-30.

ROTHBARD, Murray N. (1987): "Time Preference," in EATWELL et al. (eds. 1987), IV: 644-6.

ROTHBARD, Murray N. (1987a): "Fetter, Frank A.," in EATWELL et al. (eds. 1987), II: 308.

ROTHBARD, Murray N. (1987b): "Mises, Ludwig Edler von," in EATWELL et al. (eds. 1987), III: 479-80.

SAMUELSON, Paul S. and William D. NORDHAUS (1985): *Economics*, 12th ed., New York etc.: McGraw-Hill.

SAX, Emil (1887): *Grundlegung der theoretischen Staatswirthschaft*, Wien: Braumüller.

SCHUMPETER, Joseph A. (1954): *History of Economic Analysis*, Oxford: Oxford University Press.

SEAGER, Henry R. (1893): "Economics at Berlin and Vienna," in *Journal of Political Economy* 1, 236-62.

SEAGER, Henry R. (1912): "The Impatience Theory of Interest," in *American Economic Review* 2, 834-51.

SEAGER, Henry R. (1913): "Comment" (on FISHER 1913), in *American Economic Review* 3, 618-9.

SELGIN, George A. (1988): "Praxeology and Understanding. An Analysis of the Controversy in Austrian Economics," in *Review of Austrian Economics* 2, 19-58.

SHAND, Alexander H (1984): *The Capitalist Alternative. An Introduction to Neo-Austrian Economics*, Brighton: Wheatsheaf Books.

SPADARO, Louis M. (ed. 1978): *New Directions in Austrian Economics*, Kansas City: Sheed Andrews and McMeel.

STIGLER, George J. (1941): *Production and Distribution Theories. The Formative Period*, New York: Macmillan.

STIGLER, George J. (1966): *The Theory of Price*, 3rd ed., New York: Macmillan.

TINTNER, Gerhard (1970): "Lineare Methoden der Nationalökonomie und die Produktionsperiode von Böhm-Bawerk," in *Zeitschrift für Nationalökonomie* 30, 1-5.

TINTNER, Gerhard (1974): "Linear Economics and the Böhm-Bawerk Period of Production," in Quarterly Journal of Economics 88, 127-32.

VAUGHN, Karen I.: see MOSS and VAUGHN (1982).

VELAPILLAI, K. (1975): "Irving Fisher on 'Switches of Technique.' A Historical Note," in *Quarterly Journal of Economics* 89, 679-80.

WEBER, Wilhelm: see HICKS and WEBER (eds. 1973).

WEIZSÄCKER, Carl C. von (1971): *Steady State Capital Theory*, Berlin etc.: Springer.

WEIZSÄCKER, Carl C. von (1971a): Die zeitliche Struktur des Produktionsprozesses und das Problem der Einkommensverteilung zwischen Kapital und Arbeit," in *Weltwirtschaftliches Archiv* 106, 1-33.

WEIZSÄCKER, Carl C. von (1974): "Substitution Along the Time Axis," in *Kyklos* 27, 732-56.

WHITE, Lawrence H. (1984): Comment on GARRISON (1985), unpublished manuscript, New York University.

Wicksell, Knut (1893): *Über Wert, Kapital und Rente nach den neueren nationalökonomischen Theorien*, Jena: Fischer

WICKSELL, Knut (1924): "Mengers Grundsätze in ny upplaga," in *Economic Tidskrift*, 1-10; translated as "The New Edition of Menger's *Grundsätze*," in WICKSELL (1958), 193-203.

WICKSELL, Knut (1928): "Zur Zinstheorie (Böhm-Bawerks dritter Grund)," in MAYER et al. (eds. 1927-32), III: 199-209.

WICKSELL, Knut (1958): *Selected Papers on Economic Theory*, edited with an Introduction by Eric LINDAHL, London: Allen & Unwin.

WIESER, Friedrich von (1876): "Über das Verhältnis der Kosten zum Wert," paper presented before KNIES' Seminar at Heidelberg; published in WIESER (1929), 377-404.

WIESER, Friedrich von (1884): *Ueber den Ursprung und die Hauptgesetze des wirthschaftlichen Wertes*, Vienna: Hölder.

WIESER, Friedrich von (1889): *Der natürliche Wert*, Vienna: Hölder; translated by Christian A. MALLOCH as *Natural Value*, with an Introduction by William SMART, London: Macmillan, 1893; reprinted New York: Kelley & Milman, 1956.

WIESER, Friedrich von (1891): "The Austrian School and the Theory of Value," in Economic Journal 1, 108-21; reprinted in LITTLECHILD (ed. 1990), vol. 1, 205-18; translated into German as "Die österreichische Schule und die Werttheorie," in WIESER (1929), 35-51. (Page references are to the English reprint.)

WIESER, Friedrich von (1929): *Gesammelte Abhandlungen*, ed. Friedrich A. von HAYEK, Tübingen: Mohr.

WILLES, Mark H. (1981): "'Rational Expectations' as a Counterrevolution," in BELL and KRISTOL (eds. 1981), 81-96.

YEAGER, Leland B. (1979): "Capital Paradoxes and the Concept of Waiting," in RIZZO (ed. 1979), 187-214.

YEAGER, Leland B. (1986): "Why Subjectivism?" in *The Review of Austrian Economics* I, 5-31.

Rolf Daxhammer

Special Interest Groups and Economic Policy in Democratic Societies

Theoretical Foundations and Empirical Evidence

Frankfurt/M., Berlin, Bern, New York, Paris, Wien, 1995. 261 pp., 19 fig., 2 tab.
European University Studies: Series 5, Economics and Management. Vol. 1677
ISBN 3-631-47789-9 pb. DM 79.--*

Special Interest Groups are an integral part of economic policy decision making in democratic societies. In this book, they are to be discussed in terms of their impact on a country's economic performance. To do so the concept of a market for special privileges has to be introduced in order to develop an explicit demand/supply framework encompassing both special interest groups and political decision makers. Thus, the whole range of economists' tools can be applied to a topic that has implications not only for Economics but also for Political Science and Business Administration. The analysis opens the door for a critical assessment of recommendations that are discussed with respect to curbing and channelling the influence of special interest groups on economic policy making.

Contents: Pluralism · Formation of special interest groups (theory of collective action) · Rent-seeking · Market for special privileges (demand/supply) · Endogenous tariff theory · Policy implications

Peter Lang **Europäischer Verlag der Wissenschaften**
Frankfurt a.M. • Berlin • Bern • New York • Paris • Wien
Auslieferung: Verlag Peter Lang AG, Jupiterstr. 15, CH-3000 Bern 15
Telefon (004131) 9402121, Telefax (004131) 9402131
- Preisänderungen vorbehalten - *inklusive Mehrwertsteuer